D0607533

LOVE
IS ALL
AROUND

AND OTHER LESSONS
WE'VE LEARNED FROM

THE
MARY
TYLER
MOORE
SHOW

PAULA
BERNSTEIN

RUNNING PRESS

PHILADELPHIA

Running Press
Hachette Book Group
1290 Avenue of the Americas, New York, NY 10104
www.runningpress.com
@Running_Press

Printed in the United States

Published by Running Press, an imprint of Perseus Books, LLC,
a subsidiary of Hachette Book Group, Inc. The Running Press name and logo
is a trademark of the Hachette Book Group.

The Hachette Speakers Bureau provides a wide range of authors for speaking events.
To find out more, go to www.hachettespeakersbureau.com or call (866) 376-6591.

The publisher is not responsible for websites (or their content) that are not
owned by the publisher.

Print book cover and interior design by Frances J. Soo Ping Chow.

Library of Congress Control Number: 2020938115

ISBNs: 978-0-7624-7197-3; e-book: 978-0-7624-7196-6

LSC-C

10   9   8   7   6   5   4   3   2   1

CONTENTS

CHAPTER ONE:
OPPORTUNITY

"You can have the town—

why don't you take it?"

**—THE MARY TYLER MOORE SHOW
THEME SONG**

In one of the most memorable TV openings of all time—set to Sonny Curtis's infectious theme song, "Love Is All Around"—a fresh-faced Mary Tyler Moore, a.k.a. Mary Richards, is behind the wheel of a 1970 Ford Mustang driving toward Minneapolis and a fresh start. She's off on a new adventure, and we're right there rooting for her. Fifty years ago, Mary Richards set out to "make it on her own," and television has never been the same.

Who can forget the iconic hat toss moment at the end of the opening credits? Our plucky heroine runs into the middle of a busy intersection in downtown Minneapolis, stops, spins around, and tosses her knitted black-and-turquoise beret—some call it a tam-o'-shanter—up in the air without a care in the world. A freeze-frame captures her beaming face. The beret is forever frozen in midair. When Mary tosses her hat up in the air, she's throwing caution (or at least her hat) to the wind. She's made it this far; she's going all the way! She's taking chances, taking control of her life. She's graduating into the world as an independent woman, and her exuberance is infectious. As the seasons rolled by, the credits evolved, but Mary was always Mary. Her hopeful spirit and joie de vivre still serve as examples of how to get by in this crazy world without getting down.

With its smart writing and its flawed but lovable characters, *The Mary Tyler Moore Show* broke ground for its portrayal of a single career woman trying to "make it on her own." It is an undeniable classic—but even classics don't start out that way. Back in 1969, *The Mary Tyler Moore Show* was not much more than a name and a leading lady. Mary

Tyler Moore, the comedic actress who had won an Emmy for playing the enchanting suburban housewife Laura Petrie on *The Dick Van Dyke Show* just a few years earlier, had signed a deal with CBS to star in a sitcom. CBS had given Moore and her husband at the time, TV executive Grant Tinker, a thirteen-episode commitment, which meant there would be no pilot episode. This was jumping into the deep end of the pool before learning how to swim.

Even if you're a star of Mary Tyler Moore's caliber, that kind of opportunity only comes around once. Her attempts at stage and screen success had faltered, so she was hoping for another TV hit. This time it would be her name in the title rather than Dick Van Dyke's. Moore and Tinker got to work right away, creating their own production company, MTM Enterprises, and hiring TV writers James L. Brooks and Allan Burns. Brooks was the creator of the groundbreaking TV series *Room 222*, about a racially diverse high school history class; Burns had written a number of episodes for the Emmy Award–winning show. They were both looking to work on another innovative series— something a little edgier than most of the plain vanilla fare on TV at the time. Wholesome, rural-skewing hits like CBS's *Gunsmoke* and *Mayberry R.F.D.* were too predictable and homespun and seemed dated in the quickly changing world of the late '60s. The writers wanted to create a show that would reflect the complicated world around them—and the changing roles for women in society. Brooks and Burns had a leading lady, a title, and a deal with CBS. Now they just needed to come up with a fresh concept.

It was Moore's name in the title, but she didn't want the show to rest entirely on her shoulders. It would be an ensemble piece, and her character wouldn't be too much of a stretch from her real personality. She couldn't be married on the new show, because that would remind people of Laura Petrie. Maybe, they thought, she could have a job, like an assistant to a newspaper gossip columnist. Nah, she'd work at a TV station. Either way, the writers decided that, like *The Dick Van Dyke Show* before it, *The Mary Tyler Moore Show* would be divided between two main spheres—home and work. In their initial concept, Mary Tyler Moore would play Mary Richards, a thirty-year-old woman from small-town Minnesota who moves to Minneapolis following a divorce to "make it on her own." Brooks described *The Dick Van Dyke Show* as "people that you really liked, saying funny things frequently." *The Mary Tyler Moore Show* would aspire to do the same.

The creators had decided early on to set the show somewhere outside of New York or Los Angeles or Chicago, the typical settings for TV shows at the time. The idea of Minnesota came up after the writers were talking about the Minnesota Vikings. Minneapolis would work. The city's chilly weather would make for good plotlines—and would provide a handy excuse to film predominantly indoors (aside from some establishing exterior shots, the show was actually shot in front of a live studio audience in Hollywood, California). For Mary Richards, who came from small-town Minnesota, Minneapolis *was* the big city, which says a lot about how her character was envisioned. She was eager for adventure but wasn't going to pack up her VW Bug and drive to San Francisco.

Rather than churn out a predictable sitcom featuring yet another dutiful housewife character, writers Brooks and Burns took a chance by making the central character of Mary Richards a single career woman in her thirties. That was a bold idea at the time, given that women were just beginning to enter the workforce and there had never been a prime-time TV series centered around a single career woman. (*Julia*, which aired from 1968 to 1971, featured Diahann Carroll as a nurse and single mother, but she was a widow.) This was before *Murphy Brown, Ally McBeal, Sex and the City, Girls, 30 Rock*, and all the shows featuring single career women who followed in Mary's footsteps.

That was all fine and good, but as soon as CBS heard the word *divorce*, they freaked. Wouldn't audiences assume Moore had divorced Dick Van Dyke? She and her former on-screen spouse had had such great chemistry that TV audiences sometimes assumed they were married in real life. Besides, the CBS executives said, their research department had shared a list of taboo subjects that audiences supposedly wouldn't accept on TV, including divorce. Allan Burns later recalled: "We sat there in a room full of divorced New York Jews with mustaches and heard them say there are four things Americans don't like: New Yorkers, divorced people, men with mustaches, and Jews. It was strongly hinted that if we insisted on having Mary divorced, the show would go on at one in the morning."

So the show's creators nixed the divorced story line and settled on creating a believable backstory for Mary that would explain why she was . . . gasp! . . . single at thirty. (But they did ignore the supposed taboo about Jewish people and people from New York; the character of Rhoda is a Jew from New York.) Nowadays, nobody would bat an eyelash about a single woman at thirty. But back then, they felt the audience would wonder why our lovely heroine still hadn't tied the knot. The average age of marriage for a woman in the United States at the time was twenty, and the vast majority of adult women were married. Divorce was still considered a social stigma—and definitely not okay for America's sweetheart. So instead of a divorce, the writers explained that Mary had been dumped by her boyfriend after she supported him during his medical internship and residency. (Did they live together . . . in sin? It was hinted at but not clear.) Moore said she found the premise "incredibly distasteful, but apparently, CBS thought that was preferable to being divorced."

LIFE LESSON:
Be a Pioneer

Sometimes in order to take advantage of an opportunity, you've got to be a pioneer. *The Mary Tyler Moore Show* was groundbreaking in its depiction of a single career woman. It was groundbreaking in other ways too, pioneering what we'd now call gender diversity behind the scenes, with the highest percentage of female writers of any show at the time. In 1973, out of seventy-five freelance or staff writers for the show, twenty-five were women. For comparison, *The Partridge Family*, the show with the second-highest percentage of women writers, had only seven writers out of seventy-six. "It was unlike every other show I worked on," said writer Susan Silver. "They made a conscious decision to hire female writers because they wanted the show to reflect real women's experiences." According to Silver, Brooks and Allan "were not only eager to hear my stories, but looking for female writers, which was mostly unheard of then. I pitched stories from my own life, things that all women had experienced, but were fresh to the men."

But it wasn't just a token effort. The show creators knew that in order for it to succeed, *The Mary Tyler Moore Show* needed to tackle the issues of the day from a fresh, female perspective. Throughout the show's run, it dealt with the challenges of being a single career woman in a man's world with insight and humor. Without being overtly political, the show also took on taboo topics for TV at the time, including homosexuality, sex, birth control, and divorce, as well as hot-button issues (that, sadly, haven't changed much in the decades since) such as pay inequity. "We were never asked to be feminist writers or make political statements," said Silver. "That was more Norman Lear, *Maude, All in the Family* kind of scripts. What we were trying for, and I believe we succeeded in, was showing independent single women, working and leading their lives and supporting each other."

Love Is All Around:

The Story Behind the Theme Song

How did a singer-songwriter named Sonny Curtis come up with the catchy, inspirational theme song that set the stage for the successful series? And why did the lyrics to the show's theme song change between the first and second seasons?

It just so happened that Moore's manager also managed Curtis, whose hits included the rock and roll anthem "I Fought the Law," performed by the Bobby Fuller Four and the Clash, among other musicians.

Originally from Texas, Curtis was a bluegrass singer who played with Buddy Holly and later went on to perform with Holly's band, the Crickets, after Holly's death in 1959. When he got the call from Moore's manager, Curtis was living in LA and writing commercial jingles.

Curtis read a four-page series outline his manager had sent him and was inspired by the show's basic premise. All he knew was that it was about a young woman moving to Minneapolis and trying to make it on her own. The lyrics came to him effortlessly. "How will you make it on your own? This world is awfully big, and girl, this time you're all alone."

Curtis later told the *Los Angeles Times,* "I wrote the song in about two hours . . . that was an awfully good day for me. I remember enjoying writing that song. I just sat on my couch and took my guitar in hand and went for it. It came to me pretty quickly."

The funny thing is that Burns and Brooks hadn't even written the first episode, but somehow Curtis had come up with the perfect song to set the show's tone.

Rewatching the show, you might notice that the lyrics changed slightly between the first and second seasons.

Curtis, who also performed the song, explained, "The verse changed and the chorus stayed the same except for one line. The verse on the first show was, 'How will you make it on your own?' After the first season, [producer] Allan Burns called me and said, 'Sonny, we need a different set of lyrics, because she's obviously made it.'"

That's when Curtis came up with, "Who can turn the world on with her smile?"

Another change: on the first season, the song ends, "You might just make it after all." On the second season, that was switched to "you're gonna make it after all" because she had obviously made it.

Over the years, many artists recorded the inspirational theme song, including Sammy Davis Jr. (1976), easy listening legend Frank Chacksfield and His Orchestra (1980), Twin Cities punk rockers Hüsker Dü (1985), and Joan Jett & the Blackhearts (1996).

It's nearly impossible to listen to that song and not want to spin around and throw your hat up in the air. Try it. You'll see.

LIFE LESSON:

Take a Setback and Turn It into an Opportunity

September 19, 1970—the first episode of *The Mary Tyler Moore Show*, "Love Is All Around," introduced viewers to thirty-year-old Mary Richards and the other main characters and set the sharp, sassy tone for the show. Mary's old friend, the narcissistic but nonetheless charming Phyllis (Cloris Leachman), has found her an apartment. It seems too good to be true—and it is. Her pushy upstairs neighbor, Rhoda Morgenstern (Valerie Harper), who is eager to move out of what's essentially an attic, has already laid claim to it. Luckily for Mary, Phyllis had the foresight (or nerve, depending on how you see it) to sign the lease in Mary's name before Mary even had the chance to see it. Either way, our Mary has a new place to live! And two built-in friends.

That same day, Mary lucks out on the job-seeking front too. She initially applies for a secretarial job at local news station WJM-TV. Grizzled news producer Lou Grant (Ed Asner) tells her the job has been filled; however, there's another one available for associate producer of the 6:00 p.m. news. Mary seizes the moment. Whatever the job is, she's interested.

Mr. Grant asks her some questions that would definitely not fly nowadays. Though Mary's a natural people pleaser, she sets some limits. She only answers the personal questions that she feels like answering. He's mystified.

LOU GRANT: What religion are you?

MARY RICHARDS: Mr. Grant, I don't quite know how to say this, but you're not allowed to ask that when someone's applying for a job. It's against the law.

LOU: Wanna call a cop?

MARY: No.

LOU: Good. Would you think I was violating your civil rights if I asked if you're married?

MARY: Presbyterian.

LOU: Huh?

MARY: Well, I decided I'd answer your religion question.

Mr. Grant continues to grill her until Mary finally gets up to leave. She turns to tell Mr. Grant she's had enough of his questions. "It does seem that you've been asking a lot of very personal questions that don't have a thing to do with my qualifications for this job."

In response, Mr. Grant tells Mary, "You know what? You've got spunk . . . I hate spunk." Clearly, Mr. Grant doesn't hate spunk too much because he hires her for the job of associate producer of the 6:00 p.m. news program. Mary can't believe her good luck—until Mr. Grant announces that the associate producer job pays ten dollars less per week than the secretarial job. Still, it sounds a lot more exciting than taking transcription. She's hired! Her new coworkers include snarky but sweet news writer Murray Slaughter (Gavin MacLeod) and Ted Baxter

(Ted Knight), a pompous dolt of a news anchor. Both become part of her work family.

Back at her new home, Mary's newfound independence is tested when her ex-boyfriend shows up in Minneapolis unannounced. When he arrives at her apartment with a bouquet of flowers, she's impressed—until she learns he swiped them from a patient at the hospital where he works. Mary is underwhelmed. It's not exactly clear what he wants from her—does he want to get back together, or is he in town for a booty call? Mary gives him a chance to say what he's got to say (and maybe say he can't live without her?). When he chokes on the words *I love you*, Mary realizes she's better off without him. She says goodbye and shows him the door. As he's leaving, he tells her, "Take care of yourself."

"I think I just did," she answers.

When she arrived in Minneapolis without an apartment or a job, Mary wasn't sure what she'd find. She knew she could count on a couch at her nutty married friend Phyllis's place, but how long could she manage there without going crazy? At thirty, she had invested several years of her life in a relationship that didn't pan out. But rather than stay in small-town Minnesota with a bad boyfriend who doesn't appreciate her, she sets off for the big city of Minneapolis! The takeaway? Be like Mary Richards. If things don't go your way, take life in a new direction and be open to new opportunities. Sure, we can't all pick up and start a new life at any age, but we can at least try to see things in a fresh way.

> **MTM Trivia:** *Ted Baxter's character was one of the influences for the character Kent Brockman, the cocky anchorman on* The Simpsons, *who was developed by, among other people, James L. Brooks, the same Brooks who helped to create* The Mary Tyler Moore Show.

LIFE LESSON:

Success Sometimes Takes Time (Don't Give Up)

Five decades after it first aired, *The Mary Tyler Moore Show* is now considered a success. But as the production of the show itself illustrated, sometimes success takes time. When they performed the first episode of the show in front of a live studio audience, just days before the series premiere in 1970, the reaction was disappointing to say the least. The cast and crew later referred to the disastrous run-through as "Black Tuesday" because it seemed that everything that could go wrong did go wrong. They were experimenting with a new camera system that they hadn't quite figured out yet. The sound system was also a work in progress. It was a smoggy, 102-degree day in Los Angeles, and the air-conditioning system wasn't powerful enough to cool down the stage.

But most concerning, the audience didn't seem to get any of the jokes. Some even left halfway through the performance. Those who stayed later said that they could barely hear any of the dialogue. And what they could hear, they didn't like. They especially didn't like "that awful woman yelling at Mary," as they called Rhoda. They didn't know what to make of this pushy New Yorker who wanted to "steal" Mary's apartment. The writers had a problem: how to make the audience like Rhoda, who, to be fair, was the brassiest woman anybody had ever seen on a sitcom. She was blunt, snarky, and, worst of all, mean to Mary. Following "Black Tuesday," Moore started to panic. What had she gotten herself involved in? Tinker called the writers and ordered them to "fix it." But what could they do in only three days' time?

Script supervisor Margaret Mullen had an ingenious idea: the episode starts with Phyllis, along with her twelve-year-old daughter, Bess (Lisa Gerritsen), showing Mary the apartment and complaining about "that dumb Rhoda," who wants it for herself. Mullen suggested that Bess say something nice about Rhoda so that the audience will come to appreciate her too. The writers figured it was worth a try, so they added a line:

BESS: Aunt Rhoda's really a lot of fun! Mom hates her.

By Friday, when it was time to tape the first episode for real, they had figured out the new camera system and the faulty sound system. All the writers had done since Tuesday's disastrous run-through was tweak a couple of lines of dialogue, but that made all the difference. As Moore recalled later, "They figured out if a child liked Rhoda, then she wasn't *all* mean. There was something in her that *could* be lovable. We did the very same show and it went through the roof!"

Since the initial divorce pitch, the mustached CBS executives hadn't been fans of the show. Mike Dann, then head of programming for CBS, was focused on attracting as many viewers as possible. Who was going to be interested in a quirky comedy about a single thirty-year-old in Minnesota? He offered to buy MTM out, but Tinker said CBS would stick by its thirteen-episode deal. So Dann dumped the show into a time slot where it would be sure to fail: Tuesday nights in between rural-skewing shows *The Beverly Hillbillies* and *Hee Haw* and opposite the counterculture police drama hit *The Mod Squad*.

Things changed when Dann was pushed out of CBS and replaced with the young programming executive Fred Silverman. In the summer of 1970, soon after he took over as CBS programming chief, Silverman saw a rough cut of the first *Mary Tyler Moore* show. He was so impressed with its sophisticated humor, he immediately picked up the phone to call his boss, Bob Wood, the network president. He told Wood that the show was "wonderful" and that it had to be moved to Saturday. CBS made the unprecedented decision to shake up its prime-time schedule just a month before it was set to premiere. *The Mary Tyler Moore Show* was given a prime Saturday-night spot.

Still, success took time. The early reviews, for the most part, were bad. A *New York Times* critic called the show "preposterous" and said Moore "is caught in one ridiculous item with one set of bizarre happenings at a TV station's newsroom and another in her living accommodations." *TV Guide* said Mary was "unmarried and getting a little desperate about it," while the *St. Petersburg Times* called her a "30-year-old spinster." *Time*'s critic wrote that the show was "a disaster for the old co-star of *The Dick Van Dyke Show*" and that her coworkers in the newsroom "do an injustice to even the worst of local TV news."

The ratings were only so-so at first, barely hitting the top twenty during the first season—not great considering there were only three broadcast networks at the time. CBS was reportedly even preparing a replacement series in case they decided to pull *The Mary Tyler Moore Show*. The network made some suggestions that would take the show in a more conventional direction, with notes like, "Mary should be presented with a problem. Toward the end she should solve that problem in a surprising and comical manner."

The writers did not agree.

Rather than dumb down the show, the writers doubled down on their original concept of deriving humor from the nuanced characters they had created, not just the situation. They wouldn't subject Mary to ridiculous antics. They'd build such fully developed characters that the audience couldn't help but relate—and laugh. And as the episodes continued to deliver both real laughs and real life, the ratings improved—and CBS picked the show up for a second season.

The sitcom wasn't considered a bona fide success until the 1971 Emmy Awards—at which *The Mary Tyler Moore Show* garnered four wins and eight nominations. Critics eventually came around as audiences fell in love with the show—and, in particular, with the sassy humor and leading lady who could "turn the world on with her smile" and "take a nothing day and suddenly make it all seem worthwhile," as the lyrics of the theme song go. In 1973, the *New York Times* praised the show, which, with its "consistently tight writing and good acting" made it "the best of its kind in the history of American television." Remember, success doesn't always happen right away. You've got to give it time to develop and be discovered by others.

CHAPTER TWO

FAMILY

"What is a family anyway?
They're just people who make you feel
less alone and really loved."

—MARY RICHARDS

Family is more than the people you're raised with. Family can also be the people you choose to spend your life with. When Mary Richards sets off for Minneapolis without much more than a snazzy car, a dream of a new life in a new city, and heaps of gumption, she leaves her small-town family behind. Soon she finds the people who will become her new extended family: her work family and her home family. Mary's home family consists of her new neighbor and soon-to-be BFF, the tough, Bronx-born Rhoda Morgenstern (Valerie Harper), and Phyllis Lindstrom (Cloris Leachman), Mary's high-strung old friend turned landlady. Mary's work family includes her new boss, Lou, a.k.a. Mr. Grant, as she calls him; Murray Slaughter (Gavin MacLeod), the sarcastic news writer and Mary's office spouse; and Ted Baxter (Ted Knight), the unctuous anchorman who's the constant butt of Murray's jokes. Later, Sue Ann Nivens (Betty White), the man-eating "Happy Homemaker" arrives, as does ditzy Georgette (Georgia Engel).

This collection of oddballs seems so mismatched that it should explode, yet Mary's friends are so close-knit and at ease with each other that even though they're not related, they feel like a family. What makes them a family rather than just a bunch of acquaintances is that they are bound together by something more than a job or an apartment. They seem to really care about each other—and in turn, we care about them. As with all close families, this family looks out for each other and puts up with each other's quirks even when they're really annoying. They tend to bring out both the best and, occasionally, the worst in each other.

From early on, some critics—and armchair psychoanalysts—identified classic familial types among the show's characters. Lou, a.k.a. Mr. Grant, is the father figure, a hard-drinking, hot-tempered, but ultimately loving and supportive old-school dad. Some saw eccentric Phyllis as the crazy aunt who means well but often offends. Mary is the daughter, trying to exert independence and "make it on her own" while still relying on the support of her family. She's also the mediator who is constantly trying to keep the peace among the rest of the family. Despite being the oldest of the lead cast members, Ted is the baby of the family, used to getting his way. He'll throw a temper tantrum if he doesn't get what he wants. He's really a terror, but everybody puts up with him because he's too clueless to know better. It's easy to picture Murray as the wisecracking older brother who resents his bratty baby brother—in this case, Ted. Some see Rhoda as Mary's supportive sister in this scenario, but you could also view her as the cool older cousin who challenges Mary's narrow worldview. You know—the kind of cousin who can find where the booze is stashed and knows which party the cute guys will be at.

LIFE LESSON:

Choose Your Family

The Mary Tyler Moore Show reminds us that you need to find your family—the coworkers, friends, and neighbors who encourage you, support you, and most importantly, make you laugh. Before Mary could choose her on-screen family, the producers of *The Mary Tyler Moore Show* had to find the magical combination of people to play them. Luckily, legendary casting director Ethel Winant, who at the time was also the VP of CBS, took on their cause. She had previously cast CBS shows such as *Lost in Space, Green Acres, Hogan's Heroes, The Twilight Zone,* and *Hawaii Five-O,* and she was on her way to becoming, at least for a time, the highest-ranking female TV executive at any broadcast network. It helped to have a friend in high places. Unlike the rest of the CBS executives, who had expressed serious doubts about the show's prospects, Winant loved the few scripts she had read and wanted to boost its chances for success.

The writers knew how they wanted these characters to look, but they also knew that looks weren't as important as chemistry. Except for Mary, none of the actors who wound up getting cast looked remotely like what the writers had written in the script. Ted Baxter had been pictured as a young hunk, a potential love interest for Mary. However, when silver-haired Ted Knight, an experienced but underemployed actor—who was reportedly living paycheck to paycheck at the time— showed up at the audition wearing an anchorman-style blue blazer he'd purchased from a thrift shop, the producers couldn't help but take notice. He was much older than they'd pictured Ted Baxter, but his booming baritone voice and natural comedic timing helped him clinch the part. If anything, his age added another layer to the character as it had been written, blending a strain of insecurity with pomposity. In this way, the actors helped to shape the characters according to their own physical characteristics and unique interpretations of the roles.

MTM Trivia: *Jennifer Aniston's father, John Aniston, who at the time was starring on the soap opera* Days of Our Lives, *was considered for the role of Ted Baxter. Aniston auditioned and was called back twice, but the producers decided Ted Knight was funnier and went with him instead.*

The same was true of Valerie Harper, who in real life was way more glamorous than the frumpy Rhoda they had pictured. Harper said she was sure she wouldn't get the job because she looked too similar to Moore. "Going in, I thought it would be a bad choice. I'm a brunette like Mary and I have a small nose like Mary. I thought they'd go with someone physically different," she said. In the script, Rhoda had been described as "a self-made loser—overweight, not good with hair and makeup, and self-deprecating." After her first audition, writer and producer Allan Burns remembered thinking Harper, then working as a stage actor, was "a little prettier than we expected Rhoda to be." Before Harper auditioned for the second time, one of the show's directors suggested that she dress down and forgo makeup when she came in for her second reading. That did the trick. Harper nabbed the part. "It's a tribute to her as an actress that she was able to make herself the way the writers wanted her to look," Winant later said. Unlike her experienced costars, who were all TV veterans by this point, the show marked Harper's first—and ultimately most indelible—TV role. In fact, before *Mary Tyler Moore*, Harper didn't even have an agent and wasn't a member of the

Screen Actors Guild. Winant had seen her in a play and had her assistant track her down. Pre-internet, it took quite a bit of effort to locate her!

Gavin MacLeod was initially considered for the Lou Grant role. With his broad build and bald scalp, he had previously been typecast as a heavy. At the time they were casting the show, he was best known for his role as notorious drug pusher Big Chicken on *Hawaii Five-O*. MacLeod later said he never felt comfortable with the tough guy image and didn't think he'd be believable as Mr. Grant. When he read the script, he immediately connected with the part of Murray. The character was initially created to be Mary's office nemesis but, as played by MacLeod, was more of an everyman nice guy, or a brown bagger, as the actor called him, referring to Murray's regular brown-bag lunches. "He was going to be the one who was like a mosquito picking around at me and feeling competitive with me," Moore said of Murray's character. "Then Gavin came in and was just so warm and embracing and dear, that they felt that was a better thing to write to."

It was challenging to find the right actress for the character of Phyllis, who was her own unique blend of charismatic and crazy. At the time they were casting, Cloris Leachman was perhaps best known as the mom from the family TV show *Lassie*, not exactly what you imagine when you picture snobby, self-righteous Phyllis. "At the time, nobody thought she could do comedy," said Winant. Leachman had, in fact, only played the mother on *Lassie* for half a season and gave up the gig because she didn't find the role challenging.

Winant was confident she'd be better suited to the character of quirky, self-absorbed Phyllis. But first she had to convince the rest of the MTM gang. As Moore later recalled, Leachman made a memorable first impression. "I had never seen anything like her . . . She was just captivating and I thought to myself, she is perfect and what am I going to do with myself because she was such an electric performer. I thought I'd never be able to hold my own in a room with her." Moore's fears about being overshadowed did not stop her from hiring Leachman. The show was more important than her ego.

Aside from the role of Rhoda, Lou Grant was the toughest to cast. They needed to find an actor with enough gravitas to be believable as an intimidating boss but who could also play a teddy bear. They considered Ed Asner, a veteran TV actor, who had had his first TV role back in 1957 as part of the Golden Age of Television show *Studio One*. He had also guest starred on numerous shows throughout the 1960s, including *Route 66*, *The Untouchables*, and CBS's own *Gunsmoke*. But aside from Winant, who had faith in Asner, nobody thought he could be funny. The first time the actor read for the part of Mr. Grant, Asner could tell he flubbed the audition. Soon after he left, he returned to see if they'd give him another shot. The second time 'round, he nailed it. Show cocreator Allan Burns remembers, "We brought Mary in to read with him. They read together, and the hairs went up on the back of our necks because it was so perfect. We knew that it was great." It was that sort of natural chemistry that made the show sparkle.

Familiar Faces

Oh, hey, isn't that so-and-so? Why, yes, chances are good that it is! While streaming old episodes of *The Mary Tyler Moore Show*, see if you can spot up-and-coming talent, future prime-time stars, an award-winning singer-songwriter, and a former First Lady, among other noteworthy faces. The list of guest stars and cameos on *The Mary Tyler Moore Show* over the years is impressive. Below, in alphabetical order, we highlight some of the most memorable:

Dabney Coleman: When Mary and Lou attend a seminar in Washington, DC, Dabney Coleman plays dapper congressman Phil Whitman, Mary's date for the evening. Former First Lady Betty Ford appears in the same episode (see below). Coleman has worked steadily since then, including key roles in films such as *9 to 5*, *Tootsie*, *WarGames*, and *Stuart Little*.

Jeff Conaway: The late Conaway plays Lou's ex-girlfriend's much-younger date, Kenny Stevens, in one episode of *The Mary Tyler Moore Show*. His performance must have impressed James L. Brooks because he hired him to star as aspiring actor Bobby Wheeler on the show *Taxi*. Fans will also remember him as Kenickie from the 1978 movie *Grease* (and, in later, more challenging times, on the reality TV series *Celebrity Rehab with Dr. Drew*).

Walter Cronkite: The iconic anchorman of the *CBS Evening News* guest starred as himself in an episode where he visits the newsroom as Lou's old war buddy. When Ted Baxter meets Cronkite, he's certain the anchorman is there to offer him a network job. Dream on, Ted!

Bill Daily: After playing Major Roger Healey on *I Dream of Jeannie*, Daily guest starred as an ambitious but inept Minneapolis councilman who needs help preparing for a TV interview at WJM. That same year, Daily would land another memorable role: Howard Borden, Bob Newhart's goofy friend and neighbor on *The Bob Newhart Show*.

Jerry Van Dyke: Though Mary's old costar and on-screen spouse, Dick Van Dyke, never made an appearance on *The Mary Tyler Moore Show*, his younger brother, Jerry, who played Rob Petrie's brother on *The Dick Van Dyke Show*, did. In season 3, Mary goes on a date with the goofy Wes Callison, a comedy writer and aspiring stand-up comic played by Jerry Van Dyke. He shows up again in season 4 and proposes to Mary, but he seems desperate and self-involved, and she's (wisely) not interested in him that way.

Betty Ford: Former First Lady Betty Ford made history as the first First Lady to make a cameo appearance on a television show. When Mary and Lou attend a seminar in Washington, DC, Lou tries to impress Mary with his DC connections, but he seems to be bluffing. When he says he's on the phone with Betty Ford, she's sure he's lying. Mary tells the First Lady that her "impression of Betty Ford really stinks." Awkward!

Helen Hunt: Hunt was only fifteen when she appeared as Murray's daughter, Laurie Slaughter, in one of the final episodes of the show. She'd go on to costar in her own prime-time hit, *Mad About You*, and win an Academy Award for her performance opposite Jack Nicholson in *As Good as It Gets*.

Carole King: In the season 5 finale, "Anyone Who Hates Kids and Dogs," Mary's new beau has a son, Stevie, who is a total brat. Mary attends Stevie's birthday party and tells him what she thinks of him. Stevie's aunt Helen, played by none other than singer-songwriter Carole King (billed as Carole Larkey, using her then husband's last name), doesn't appreciate Mary's honesty.

Bernie Kopell: Bernie Kopell, who played Mary's date Tony Kramer in season 5 of *The Mary Tyler Moore Show*, would later costar with Gavin MacLeod (Murray Slaughter) for ten seasons of *The Love Boat* (1977), on which he played the ship's doctor.

Craig T. Nelson: You may know him as Coach, the lead in the TV series of the same name, or as Zeek Braverman on *Parenthood*, or as any of his other memorable roles (*Young Sheldon, My Name Is Earl, Poltergeist*). In only his second professional role, back before he used his middle initial, Nelson appeared as Charlie, a flirty young mechanic working on Mary Richards's car in season 3.

John Ritter: In 1975, two years before he became a star as Jack Tripper on *Three's Company*, Ritter appeared on *The Mary Tyler Moore Show* as the young tennis-playing reverend who marries

Ted and Georgette in his tennis whites. He followed that up with appearances on the MTM spin-offs *Rhoda* and *Phyllis*, as well as *The Love Boat*, alongside Bernie Kopell (see above) and Gavin MacLeod (Murray Slaughter).

Doris Roberts: Long before everyone loved her as Raymond's mother on *Everybody Loves Raymond*, Doris Roberts tried to help Phyllis find a job in the episode "Phyllis Whips Inflation."

Penny Marshall: The future costar of *Laverne and Shirley* and film director (*A League of Their Own*) played a new neighbor of Mary's who is set up on a date with Lou in order to make his ex-girlfriend jealous.

Isabel Sanford: A Minneapolis councilman (played by Bill Daily) needs a whole lot of help for a TV interview at WJM. Sanford, the future matriarch on *The Jeffersons*, plays the mother of one of the councilman's staff members.

Henry Winkler: Before he was the Fonz on *Happy Days* and, much later, the acting coach on HBO's *Barry*, Winkler showed up as Steve Waldman, Rhoda's date and an unexpected guest for yet another one of Mary's failed parties. When the party guests ask, "How are you?" he replies, "I was just fired."

LIFE LESSON:

Set Healthy Boundaries with Your Family Members

Most families are dysfunctional, but some families are more dysfunctional than others. Either way, if you're going to spend the bulk of your time with these people, you're going to need to establish some healthy boundaries. The tricky part is figuring out what's healthy. Even when you set a boundary, you can be somewhat flexible, depending on the circumstances, right? You don't have to react to every snide comment or offensive joke. Sometimes it's okay to let little things slide—or else you'll be constantly irritated. There's a time to hold someone close, and there's a time to go into the other room and cool off a bit.

As much as the constellation of characters on the show felt like a family, the characters also had real family members who would show up from time to time and make life particularly challenging. The second script that Brooks and Burns wrote involved one such occasion, when Rhoda's overbearing Jewish mother, Ida Morgenstern (Nancy Walker), shows up unannounced, and Rhoda refuses to see her. CBS objected to that plotline. The network didn't think audiences approved of Jews on TV in the first place—and who would treat their mother that way? If audiences had trouble with the way Rhoda talked to Mary, they certainly wouldn't appreciate her avoiding her mother.

Though the network didn't understand what the writers were going for, Tinker did. He told them that CBS "can tell you not to shoot it, but they can't stop you." They shot the episode against CBS's wishes. It was the right call. In the end, Walker would win an Emmy for that episode—and it highlighted a new kind of family relationship for prime time. Explaining why she refuses to see her mother, Rhoda tells Mary, "It's a Jewish kind of love. I'm talking about Bronx love. There's a certain amount of guilt that goes with that." Ida is tiny but domineering. As Rhoda puts it, "I was five years old before I knew my father could talk. You know the first thing he said? 'Listen to your mother.'"

Throughout the series, Rhoda's parents occasionally pop in, but Rhoda learns to put up with them. She also learns to create boundaries so they don't drive her crazy. In one episode, Ida hangs out with Rhoda and Mary and tries to be one of the girls. She even buys a dress to match Rhoda's and takes off her bra so she can be with it. Rhoda wisely sets limits and tells her mother she doesn't want her as a girlfriend—and orders her to put her bra back on!

Even though Mary can't understand the "Jewish kind of love" Rhoda is talking about, she can relate to the need to create boundaries with one's parents. When Mary's WASPish parents move to Minneapolis, suddenly, they're a little too close for comfort. One time, when she doesn't get home until the early hours of the morning, her mother checks in on her and asks where she spent the night. Mary very firmly refuses to answer, saying she's an adult and it's none of her business. Maybe she learned a thing or two about boundaries from Rhoda.

As the seasons progress, Mary gets better at setting limits. But it's a constant struggle for Mary to say no. She's terrified of hurting people's feelings. Still, her innate decency ensures that she'll say no if a friend is asking for something illegal, like, for instance, when Ted Baxter is audited and asks Mary to lie to the IRS for him. Mary's not *that* much of a pushover!

LIFE LESSON:
Remember That People—and Relationships—Change

It was the 1970s, and social mores were changing—fast. Though the network executives had initially nixed the idea of Mary being divorced, the writers decided to tackle the subject from a new perspective. In an episode toward the end of the opening season, we learn that Lou and his wife, Edie (Priscilla Morrill), have separated and are seeing a marriage counselor. The writers continued to thread that story line for two seasons—with the couple getting back together and separated again—until they finally get divorced in season 4. At the time, it was rare for sitcoms to tackle serious topics, and it was also unusual for a story line to carry through over many episodes. Remember—this was way before binge-watching and DVRing.

Though the show was first and foremost a comedy, the writers allowed the characters they created to grow and change, often injecting an element of pathos into the humor. Watching the show, it was not unusual to go from laughing to crying within moments. Since viewers had gotten to know and care about the Grants' marriage, the episode "The Lou and Edie Story" was emotionally powerful. Through his anger over Edie's decision to leave him, Lou is wounded and confused. He asks, "How can you leave me, Edie?" The scene that follows helped earn the episode a 1973 Emmy Award for its writing. Edie explains her decision:

> **EDIE:** When I married you, I was nineteen years old, and I thought you were the most wonderful man I ever met. I still think so. But I want to learn more about the rest of me. Not just the part that's your wife. I may hate it, and I may screw it up, but I want to have time to get to know Edie MacKenzie Grant.

Thanks, in part, to the burgeoning women's movement, women who had married young started to realize there was more to life than being someone's devoted wife. But while divorce was becoming more common off-screen, it was still a rarity in prime time. It certainly had never been tackled with such nuance and sensitivity before. Audiences and critics alike applauded the realistic representation of divorce—and the show's ability to confound expectations. "On MTM, characters developed, changed, sometimes in ways disconcerting to all those schooled in the inevitability of happy endings," *Time* magazine later noted.

Compared to the idealized sitcom marriages portrayed previously on *The Dick Van Dyke Show* and before that on *I Love Lucy, Leave It to Beaver,* and other hit shows, *The Mary Tyler Moore Show* acknowledged that marriages were complicated—and divorce was an option. The show also took on issues of infertility and adoption with story lines involving Ted and Georgette and Murray and his wife, Marie. The show reflected the time period when traditions, including family, were changing. Who's to say what defines a family anyway?

CHAPTER THREE:
FRIENDS

"Hey, Rhoda, do you know what I'm doing?
I am changing my clothes at eight o'clock
at night so that I can go to a club where
I'm going to lie about being divorced so that
I can perhaps in a few months' time end up
in Paris speaking Spanish."

—MARY RICHARDS

Just as it did with family, *The Mary Tyler Moore Show* expanded the definition of friendship on TV. It was as much about friendship as it was about work and love. The show explored friendships of all varieties, including female friendship, work friends, frenemies (though the term wasn't around yet), needy friends, old friends, new friends, and friends who want to be more than friends. Mary had her BFF, Rhoda, her work spouse, Murray, and her old friend, Phyllis, who often behaved more like a frenemy. Then, in later seasons, Mary found a new frenemy in Sue Ann Nivens (Betty White) and a sweet new friend in Georgette. Along the way there was Mr. Grant, Mary's boss, who over the years became a trusted friend—and for one awkward episode, maybe something more?

Just like in real life, the relationships on the show are occasionally messy—even BFFs Mary and Rhoda have some pretty big fights, and that's not including when they argue over the dirty dishes in the sink. Mean girls Phyllis and Sue Ann are constantly putting Mary down in subtle, passive-aggressive ways, but Mary never lets it get to her. Ted is the clueless, self-involved friend nobody wants to hang out with, the butt of the bulk of the jokes. Ted is such a blockhead that he doesn't seem to understand that everybody is laughing at him. Despite it all, Mary and the office gang show up when Ted is in a jam—like the time he gets suckered into donating money to a fake journalism school named after him. His friends pretend to be the school faculty to satisfy the one student who's enrolled. Now *that's* friendship!

Mary is a devoted friend—some might even say she's too devoted. It seems like almost every episode she helps solve a different friend's problem. She is always there for her friends when they need her, though her help often backfires. As in life, none of the characters are perfect, nor are their friendships. Their flaws are what make them so relatable—and all these years later, so memorable. Together, with all their foibles, the ragtag group of friends amounts to much more than the sum of its parts. Their quirky characteristics and unlikely friendships helped to generate episode ideas. The genius of the show's writers is that they took all this interpersonal tension and put it to work in a comedy.

LIFE LESSON:

When It Comes to BFFs, Opposites Attract

It's a proven fact: the less alike two friends are, the easier they'll get along. Maybe opposites attract because they keep things interesting. They're always being exposed to new perspectives. Why hang out with someone who is just like you? You'd agree on everything, which gets tired real fast. One 2015 academic study analyzed combinations of people who became best friends and concluded that the relationships actually thrived *because* of their individual differences.

"Friendships work best with a certain amount of opposite attracting. This makes it different from a romantic relationship, where it helps if you are largely similar," the study's researcher concluded. That might help explain why mismatched BFFs Rhoda and Mary work so well together—though that wasn't initially the case. In fact, their first meeting in the series premiere occurs in the first few minutes of the first episode, and it's more of a straight-on confrontation with the two women competing for the same apartment.

Rhoda's first words to Mary are, "Hello. Get out of my apartment." Rhoda is New York Jewish to Mary's Minnesota WASP nice and doesn't tone down her New York attitude for this Minneapolis newbie. Mary quickly sizes up the situation: "You think I'm some kind of pushover, don't you?" Mary says. "Well, then you're in for a little surprise because if you push me, then I just might have to push back—hard."

Rhoda cracks up laughing. "Come on," she replies, laughing in Mary's face. "You can't carry that off."

"I know," Mary admits, rolling her eyes.

Thanks to her frenemy Phyllis, who had the foresight (and the nerve) to sign the apartment lease before Mary even saw it, Mary ends up with the sweet bachelorette pad. Luckily, Rhoda lives upstairs, so they'll almost be like roommates. "In spite of everything, you're really a pretty hard person to dislike," Mary tells Rhoda.

Rhoda replies, "I know what you mean. I'm having a pretty hard time hating you as well. We'll both have to work on it." By the second episode, they're already BFFs.

From the beginning, the writers envisioned the characters as unlikely friends who could hardly be more different. As *Newsweek* put it back in 1973, Rhoda is "a brassy contrast to the squarer, slightly uptight Mary Richards." Mary is Minnesota nice, and Rhoda is New Yawk attitude. Harper later said, "Mary had this politeness and squareness about her. But Rhoda was Rhoda. She was a kick in the butt." While Mary assumes the best of everyone, Rhoda believes the worst. Rhoda is self-deprecating and obsessed with the idea of getting married, whereas Mary is confident and in no rush to partner up. While Mary has a tendency to be indecisive and thoughtful, Rhoda tends to be impetuous. She seizes the moment, which can, occasionally, lead to some awkward situations, like when Rhoda brings a guy she just met to a seated dinner party of Mary's where there's not enough food for him. Or when Rhoda uses the money she borrows from Mary to buy her a car—without asking her first. But she means well, so it's hard to be angry—but why did she have to pick a yellow car?

Rhoda is constantly berating her looks and comparing herself unfavorably to Mary, the annoying friend who manages to look fabulous in whatever outfit she throws on at the last minute. Of course, looking back at the show now, it's apparent that Rhoda was fabulous in her own right. But she couldn't stop putting herself down with comic one-liners. When offered a piece of candy, Rhoda replies, "I don't know whether to eat this or apply it directly to my hips.".

> **RHODA:** How can you gorge yourself and stay so skinny? I'm so hungry I can't stand it.
>
> **MARY:** Why don't you eat something?
>
> **RHODA:** I can't. I've got to lose ten pounds by eight thirty.

Rhoda is always on the lookout for a date—and a mate. "There was a time when I went to bed thinking, 'Well, there goes another day not married.' Now, I just wait till New Year's Eve and say, 'There goes another year not married.' Mary, I tell you, it's progress." Though the two friends bond over being single women in their thirties, Rhoda's reached the point of desperation over it. "What am I? I'm not married. I'm not engaged. I'm not even pinned. I bet Hallmark doesn't even have a card for me!" Rhoda complains. Yet somehow it seems that every male character who meets Mary is immediately hypnotized by her beauty and charms, including, occasionally, Rhoda's dates!

Next to Mary, Rhoda feels like chopped liver. With her low self-esteem, Rhoda sees her job as a window dresser at a department store as insignificant compared to Mary's job as associate producer of the 6:00 p.m. news. "You've got the kind of job Gloria Steinem would applaud," Rhoda says to Mary before predictably putting her own job down. Rhoda often envies Mary's life, dropping lines like, "Sometimes I think you live in a shampoo commercial." Flipping through Mary's photo album, Rhoda asks, "Could I have it? I'd like to leave it in my apartment and have people think it was my life." Rhoda sometimes seems in awe of Mary and what she sees as the perfect life. As Harper said in an interview with the Archive of American Television in 2009, "Rhoda felt inferior to Mary. Rhoda wished she was Mary. Rhoda looked up to her. All I could do was, not being as pretty, as thin, as accomplished, was: 'I'm a New Yorker, and I'm going to straighten this shiksa out.'"

In the episode "Put on a Happy Face," Mary, who generally seems to glide through life without any disappointments or setbacks, suddenly has a streak of bad luck—all in one day. Her car gets a flat tire, so she's late to work. She spills coffee on her brand-new sweater. Her date for the Teddy Awards cancels at the last minute. She accidentally tosses the obituary file. She falls and sprains her foot, *and* she catches a cold. And that's not all of it! Just as Mary begins to complain to Rhoda, Rhoda tries to top her with tales of her own flat tires. Rhoda's not used to having to listen to Mary complain! Mary never has anything to complain about! "Rhoda, would you mind? Would you just give someone else a chance to be the most miserable, just once in a while?"

Just as things are going off the rails for Mary, Rhoda's got a string of good fortune, including a new boyfriend. But, as Rhoda points out, Mary's luck will improve because . . . she's Mary. "You're not the crummy-life type. I am the crummy-life type. You're having a lousy streak. I happen to be having a terrific streak. Soon the world will be back to normal again. Tomorrow you will meet a crown head of Europe and marry. I will have a fat attack, eat three hundred peanut butter cups, and die."

Rhoda is a straight shooter, not one to beat around the bush, a perfect foil for a woman whose biggest fear is hurting someone's feelings. As Harper later told NPR's *Talk of the Nation*, "Rhoda had a wonderful quality of saying the unsayable, things that Mary Richards would not say because she's too much of a lady, or you know, it's not polite. Rhoda, the New Yorker from the Bronx, would just say it straight out." For two BFFs, Mary and Rhoda disagree a lot. But they're also looking out for each other. As the show's writers put it, Mary's relationship with Rhoda "was the constant blend of affection and conflict." The two friends start out with preconceptions about each other but end up bonding over shared experiences and growing closer. They seem to bring out the best in each other, as any BFFs should.

LIFE LESSON:

Stand Up for Your Friends

What's a good friend if not someone who will have your back when you need it? Even though they don't always get along, the characters on *The Mary Tyler Moore Show* are there for each other when it really matters. In the second season episode "Some of My Best Friends Are Rhoda," Mary and her preppy new friend, Joanne, need an extra player for their tennis game. Mary suggests Rhoda, but Joanne explains that Rhoda can't join their game, because her country club doesn't permit Jews. Joanne says she finds the club policy offensive, but it hasn't been a problem, because she doesn't know any Jews. Mary encourages Joanne to get to know Rhoda and see how wrong the club's policy is. But Joanne doesn't want to get to know Rhoda, because, well, she's Jewish. Mary says she can't go to the club either, because, ahem, she's also Jewish. Joanne doesn't quite believe that WASPish Mary is Jewish—who would?—but regardless, she gets the message. She and Mary won't continue to be tennis partners—or friends. It was probably the most heavy-handed, message-oriented episode of the series, but it certainly revealed how far Mary would go to stand up for a friend.

Sometimes standing up for your friends means standing up *to* your friends. In the season 1 episode "Bess, You Is My Daughter Now," Mary babysits for Phyllis's precocious twelve-year-old daughter, Bess (Lisa Gerritsen). Phyllis, who parents by the book (the childcare book, that is) tells Mary to study up so she can understand Bess. But when Mary ditches the books in favor of a fun day in Minneapolis, Bess has such a relaxed, wonderful time that she doesn't want to go home to her domineering mother. Neurotic, competitive Phyllis, who prides herself on being perfect at everything, is distraught that Mary seems to be better at parenting than she is. It's not easy, but Mary tells Phyllis what she thinks she needs to hear: "I'm trying to figure out a nice way to say I think you're a lousy mother." Rather than just dumping on her friend, Mary tries to support Phyllis with honest advice: stop striving to be perfect. Mary explains that sometimes Phyllis can come on too strong—and that it's okay if she shows some vulnerability. "I like you so much better when you come on weak," Mary says. Her message mostly gets across to Phyllis, who lets down her guard a little bit with Bess, who happily goes back home with her. Sometimes being a friend means telling your friend they need an attitude adjustment.

When actress Georgia Engel was hired to play Georgette Franklin, a soft-spoken, baby-faced coworker of Rhoda's in season 3, it added a new type of friend to the group. Engel had been signed on for just one episode, but her sweet-natured, space-case character so impressed the writers that the role soon expanded. The producers decided the actress would make an ideal love interest for Ted Baxter. Her high-pitched voice and ethereal demeanor seemed the perfect contrast to Ted's bluster and might bring out his softer side. After Ted starts dating the devoted and naive Georgette, Mary and Rhoda notice how he doesn't treat her very well. Georgette's new friends urge her to stand up for herself. The women's lib pep talk seems to do the trick because Georgette tells Ted not only that she won't do his laundry anymore but also that she wants him to stop calling her *baby*. "I'm not a baby," she says firmly. He comes up with some alternatives: "cookie, honey, lambkins, angelpuss, ducky— or something that Murray can come up with." She asks him to call her Georgette, and he agrees to her terms. Good thing her friends have her back!

> **MTM Trivia:** *Georgia Engel was twenty-five years younger than Ted Knight, her on-screen spouse. The large age gap and the skewed power dynamic in the relationship might draw scrutiny nowadays.*

LIFE LESSON:
Don't Let Frenemies Bring You Down

What is a frenemy except a friend who sometimes seems more like an enemy? With her nonstop self-aggrandizement and snarky comments about Mary's single status, smugly married Phyllis is the prototypical self-absorbed frenemy. Looking perfectly coiffed, Phyllis swoops into Mary's apartment regularly, boasting about "being a model wife and a perfect mother." Rhoda snipes, "She's going to give overbearing, aggressive women a bad name." Phyllis is the self-appointed expert in everything and is happy to provide advice—even if you don't want it. She is constantly putting Mary down in passive-aggressive ways. "When a girl is almost thirty and attractive, I find it hard to understand how she isn't married," Phyllis tells Mary. She regularly asks favors of Mary—such as teaching Bess about the birds and the bees!—and she refuses to take no for an answer. "You're just *so Mary*," she says, as if somehow that alone is an insult.

Phyllis views Mary through her own judgmental, competitive lens. But the amazing thing is Mary doesn't let it bother her. She smiles and nods her head, occasionally coming up with a snappy retort to one of Phyllis's insults. Instead of getting sucked into Phyllis's power plays, Mary opts to focus on the friend part of their relationship and laugh off the rest. It's a good reminder that if you don't feed the drama, the frenemy will usually back off—or at least stop seeing you as a rival. On the other hand, Phyllis and Rhoda were always an explosive combination, starting with the first episode. They're always at each other's necks. Rhoda, unlike Mary, is never one to back down from a confrontation, and Phyllis isn't one to be outdone. The two of them always have the perfect comeback.

PHYLLIS: Believe it or not, I too once had a feeling of inadequacy.

RHODA: Oh, no. We're not going to hear about your honeymoon again, are we?

With Phyllis and Rhoda getting ready to leave the show for their own spin-off series, the producers thought it was time to introduce a new female character. They came up with Sue Ann Nivens, who was described in the script as "a man-eating bitch who laid out her victims with the sweetness of a Betty White." If they want a Betty White–type, Moore said, they should cast Betty White herself. And so they did.

In "The Lars Affairs," the first episode of the show's fourth season, White makes her first appearance as Sue Ann Nivens, the passive-aggressive and oh-so-perky host of the *Happy Homemaker* show on WJM. On air, she's syrupy sweet, but when she's off air, she's a barracuda. It doesn't take long to see that there's a new frenemy in town—and she's not just a homemaker; she's a homewrecker! Sue Ann sleeps with Phyllis's husband, the never-seen but often-discussed dermatologist, Dr. Lars Lindstrom. Phyllis discovers the truth (when he comes home with cleaner clothes than when he left), and she threatens to "rip Sue Ann's face off." Phyllis confronts Sue Ann, who happens to be taping an episode of her show on how to bake a chocolate soufflé. Slamming the oven door shut, Phyllis causes the soufflé to fall. A horrified Sue Ann removes the destroyed soufflé from the oven and (in an improvised move that Betty White came up with) bumps the oven door shut with her knee and howls, "Oh, my poor baby!"

But here's the kicker—she's just tried to steal Phyllis's husband, and Sue Ann is the one who is outraged. "Now, what did that soufflé ever do to you?" she asks Phyllis accusingly. "There was no need for violence. Why you should deliberately destroy an innocent soufflé that never did you any harm is beyond me. I think you've gone too far!" Phyllis was not expecting things to go this way at all.

"You're bananas, you know that?" Phyllis says to Sue Ann. Sue Ann still has no plans to give up Lars until Mary gives her an ultimatum: if word gets out the "Happy Homemaker" is a homewrecker, it won't be good for ratings. Ever the opportunist, Sue Ann agrees to the deal, for the sake of her fans, of course. The episode ends with Phyllis asking if Sue Ann knows how to remove chocolate stains. When she says she does, Phyllis flings the remainder of the chocolate soufflé all over Sue Ann's frilly white apron. That'll teach her a lesson . . . for the moment.

Even most hardcore fans of *The Mary Tyler Moore Show* have a hard time believing that the memorable Sue Ann character didn't appear until season 4 of the series—and was initially hired for only a single episode. The producers had wrongly assumed that audiences wouldn't accept such a backstabbing, man-stealing character. But, as Moore put it, White's performance of Sue Ann was "so great, so inventive that you couldn't not have her back on." Moore noted that the character became a fan favorite and "everyone's delicious pixie" because "she represented all the little evil corners and dark places that we have inside us. And they cheered her on." After her first juicy appearance went so swimmingly, the producers asked White to clear her schedule since they wanted her to become a series regular.

Throughout the rest of the show's run, Sue Ann continues to be self-absorbed, sex crazed, and predatory—in the most entertaining way. Her character just becomes more blatantly outrageous; at one point, she risks her colleagues' lives by knowingly feeding them curdled custard rolls. Still, how could you not laugh at Sue Ann's perkiness as she announces the ludicrous segments of *The Happy Homemaker*, such as "What's all this fuss about famine?" and "Why date a dud when you could grab a stud?" Like Phyllis, Sue Ann loves to point out what she sees as people's weaknesses. This is typical frenemy behavior. When Mary gets promoted to producer, Sue Ann seems surprised. Only Sue Ann could somehow turn the good news into a zinger of an insult: "Mary, believe me. I'm proud that you haven't been disheartened by those who murmur that you've sacrificed your femininity to your ambition." Mary doesn't let Sue Ann's passive-aggressive remarks bother her. She rolls her eyes and laughs it off—always the best way to handle a frenemy.

Later in the series, when Sue Ann is looking to hire an assistant producer for her show, she "compliments" Mary: "You'd be perfect. You're a freethinking, independent, unshackled woman, exactly the kind of person to jump when I whistle." Mary knows better than to work for Sue Ann—or react to this passive-aggressive swipe. She lets it slide.

The unique friend relationships of *The Mary Tyler Moore Show* shifted from seasons 1 to 4, which featured Rhoda and Phyllis, and seasons 4 to 7, which featured Sue Ann and Georgette. All four actresses appear in season 4, which you might say marks the unofficial passing of the frenemy torch from Phyllis to Sue Ann. Once Rhoda and Phyllis leave the show, it switches focus. While it had previously balanced plotlines between Mary's home family and work family, after season 4, it became primarily a show about Mary's work family.

QUIZ: Are You the Mary or the Rhoda?

1. Your mother's coming to visit. Do you:

   a) decide to go on vacation?

   b) clean your apartment?

   c) hide in your apartment?

   d) make sure you're looking your best?

2. People describe you as:

   a) perky

   b) pushy

   c) nice

   d) sarcastic

3. You're late for work. Do you:

   a) hurry up and get going?

   b) stop and talk a little?

   c) try on a few more outfits?

   d) rush out the door looking fabulous?

4. You'd describe your childhood as:

   a) idyllic

   b) happy

   c) rough

   d) You don't want to hear about it!

5. You would describe your style as:

    a) hippie chic

    b) classic

    c) office professional

    d) boho

6. You're never fully dressed without a(n):

    a) smile

    b) attitude

    c) sweater set

    d) head scarf

7. People sometimes call you out for being too:

    a) aggressive

    b) nice

    c) passive-aggressive

    d) blunt

8. When a friend offends you, you:

    a) let it go. They probably didn't mean it.

    b) demand an apology.

    c) say something offensive back to them.

    d) roll your eyes and hope they get the message.

9. Your biggest fear is:

    a) hurting someone's feelings.

    b) being single.

    c) not being able to express yourself.

    d) not finding the perfect thing to wear.

10. Your dream job is:

    a) TV producer

    b) window dresser

    c) journalist

    d) wife

Add up your responses.

If more than five of your answers were "Rhoda," then you're the Rhoda! You're smart, sassy, and have your own unique style. You put yourself down more than you should, but you also bring a fun and open attitude to everything you do. You're a faithful friend, and your pals know they can count on you to be straight with them. You're gonna make it after all!

If more than five of your answers were "Mary," then you're the Mary! You're a smart, overachieving good girl who likes to play by the rules. You're always there for your friends and family when they need you, but you're not afraid to set healthy limits. You're confident in yourself and curious about the world. You're gonna make it after all!

CHAPTER FOUR:
WORK

"If I don't like you, I'll fire you!
If you don't like me, I'll fire you!"

—LOU GRANT

A s with many jobs, the most challenging part of Mary Richards's job isn't the work itself; it's having to deal with her coworkers. She's the only woman in the newsroom and, often, the lone voice of reason. She plays the unofficial role of office mediator, smoothing over everyone else's bumps. When Mr. Grant blows a gasket, she's the one who tells him to knock it off. When the usually egotistical Ted has a rare moment of self-doubt and fears he'll be replaced, Mary gives him a boost of confidence. When Ted mangles Murray's artfully written copy on the 6:00 p.m. news, it's Mary who cools things between them, not that Ted really had much clue what was going on. Remember—this is the guy who has a hard time pronouncing *Chicago*.

Compared to Ted, who is constantly running his mouth off about something stupid, and Mr. Grant, who is often barking orders, Murray is a relatively low-maintenance coworker. He's more sensitive than the other guys in the office, but his constant negativity and snarkiness can get tired real fast. He's a good listener, and also a good gossiper, and not the best at keeping secrets. Then in season 4, Sue Ann, a.k.a. the Happy Homemaker, arrives with her innuendos and snide remarks. She's worse than the guys. But somehow, Mary doesn't let it get to her, even when Sue Ann says things like, "Oh, dear, sweet, innocent Mary," in the most condescending way.

Mary sees the best in people and doesn't let her coworkers' annoying quirks and personality flaws drive her crazy—although sometimes it's not so easy! She also knows that there's more to each of her coworkers than their most annoying traits, a good lesson for anyone with coworkers. Even though her coworkers occasionally drive her batty, she cares about them and treats them with respect. Sometimes she's too understanding. It clearly annoys Sue Ann, who tells her, "Mary, you help everyone with his problems. You get a lot of credit for it too, affection even. And now you must help me prove that I can be a giving, under-standing, sympathetic person like you. If you don't, I'll turn on you like that (snaps fingers)!"

Though it takes her time to grow into the role of associate producer, and later, producer, Mary is totally competent, a real grown-up (maybe the only one in the room). Her coworkers know they can count on her to show up for them. When new management comes in and axes Mr. Grant, it's Mary who heads to see the eccentric cowboy star–turned–station owner Wild Jack Monroe (played by cowboy-turned-actor Slim Pickens) to get his job back—and she succeeds. "I suppose you feel like Mary Pop-pins or something," Mr. Grant says. That's his way of saying, "Thank you."

Despite her natural people-pleasing tendencies, Mary learns to assert herself at work and to put Ted in his place. In time, she becomes a real boss lady! Here are just a few of the life lessons we can learn from Mary's experience in the WJM newsroom:

LIFE LESSON:
Learn to Take Charge

It's hard to take charge if you don't think you deserve the opportunity you're given. Mary Richards has a serious case of what we'd now call imposter syndrome. She doesn't think she deserves her job, and early on, she seems reluctant to assert herself. One time, when she's put in charge of the office and someone calls asking for the boss, she places them on hold, takes a moment, and then answers in a deep voice, pretending to be a man. Some of that insecurity probably stems from the fact she had initially applied for the secretary job but was handed the associate producer job without any prior experience. But it also reflects the reality of the times, when it was rare for a woman to work in a TV newsroom. In fact, it was rare for a woman to have any job aside from nurse, teacher, or secretary. And then after getting married and having kids—because that was, of course, the ultimate goal—you were expected to stay home and be a housewife, like Laura Petrie. So it's totally understandable that Mary wouldn't be confident in her new role.

At first, she's got a big title but no responsibilities to go with it. When she's initially hired as associate producer, she assumes she'll be busy with meaningful work. Instead, on her first day at WJM, she's left to sharpen pencils. When she finishes sharpening pencils, she starts breaking pencils so she'll have something else to do. She asks her new boss, Mr. Grant, for something to keep her busy, and he tells her, "I'm too busy to keep you busy."

She asks her new coworker why Mr. Grant hired her if he doesn't have work for her to do. "Maybe he was bombed," Murray replies. Mary looks shocked. "No, I mean it," insists Murray.

Mary's not sure what to make of his comment, but she realizes that if she's going to make it in this job, she's going to have to learn how to deal with her gruff, maybe-bombed boss and kooky coworkers. But more than that, she's going to have to go out of her comfort zone and learn to speak up and take charge.

Taking charge doesn't come easily to Mary Richards, but she learns to do it when she has no other choice. During a snowstorm on a local election night, the phone lines go down, and Mr. Grant forces Mary to take charge of the newsroom. "You want me to be in charge? But that's your job," she says, stuttering. "No, my job is telling you what your job is." Mary tells Mr. Grant that she's not good at being a boss. "In order to be in charge, you have to be able to assert authority, and I've just never been any good at that." (Note: Do not say this to your boss.) Lou has no time or patience for Mary's insecurity.

She heads to the set preparing to give instructions, but she struggles to find the courage to order anyone around. Instead, she apologetically whispers, "I'm sort of in charge of the show tonight." Not surprisingly, the crew ignores her. But by the end of the episode, when everyone in the newsroom is ready to call the election so they can go home after a long night, Mary asserts authority. They haven't yet heard the official results, and Mary doesn't want to risk announcing the wrong winner. She tells Ted that if he declares a winner on-air, he's fired. He can't tell if she's bluffing, but he doesn't risk it. Her strategy works, and for once, Ted doesn't say the wrong thing. "I just opened my mouth and 'you're fired' came out. I guess I'm not so bad at being in charge after all," Mary tells Rhoda.

By season 4, Mary again asks for more responsibilities. "Mr. Grant, after working here for three years and doing every little piddly job from ordering paper clips to tweezers, I think I'm ready for a little more responsibility, something challenging, something difficult." He wants her to hire a new sportscaster, but first she's got to fire the old sportscaster, Ed Kavanagh. She balks at that. "I've never fired anyone in my life. I had a cleaning lady once I couldn't fire, so I moved!"

She takes Ed to lunch, thinking it will soften the blow, but he gets the wrong idea and thinks she's hitting on him. He wraps his arm around her shoulder, and when she tries to fire him, he won't let her get a word in edgewise. "Why don't you just let me take it from here on in?" he asks Mary, taking her hand and kissing it.

She's left with no choice but to give it to him straight: "Ed, you're fired."

He thinks she's joking. He starts laughing and continues to kiss her hand. When he realizes she's not kidding, he's not having it. His male ego is threatened. "No broad is going to fire Ed Kavanagh. How about that?"

Mary is pissed. "Well, Ed, you're fired. A broad just fired you." You go, girl!

Mary works her way up to producer by season 5, but she still has to push for more responsibilities to accompany the title. She doesn't wait for Mr. Grant to give her these responsibilities, nor does she go ahead and take them on her own. In typical Mary fashion, and true to the time, Mary asks very politely, "Since you've made me a producer a week ago, I just feel I should be doing more. Supervising somebody. Can't you give me something to do? I don't care how small or insignificant." He asks her to fix his desk chair. Now that's just rude. "Mr. Grant, I am not a chair-squeak fixer," she says. "I'm the producer." Damn straight you are! Mary may not have shattered the glass ceiling, but at least she cracked it.

MTM Trivia: *The show's producers originally considered actor Jack Klugman for the role of Lou Grant, but he had already committed to the role of Oscar Madison on* The Odd Couple. *Adapted from the hit Neil Simon play, the sitcom premiered just six months after* The Mary Tyler Moore Show.

LIFE LESSON:

Stand Up to Your Boss (When Necessary)

From their very first scene together, where he tells her, "You've got spunk . . . I hate spunk," Mary's relationship with her boss, Mr. Grant, is . . . complicated. First off, everyone calls him Lou except for Mary, who insists on calling him Mr. Grant. Secondly, Mr. Grant treats Mary like a secretary and sometimes as an office wife, asking her to make his coffee, buy his wife a birthday present, and, once he's divorced, drop off his suits at the cleaners. He proudly declares himself a "male chauvinist pig" and dares her to disagree with him.

But Mary has a way of getting through to Mr. Grant. She's always knocking on his office door and asking, "Mr. Grant, can I talk to you for a moment?" She doesn't yell or play up to his ego. Her voice quavers, and she occasionally breaks down crying, but she does manage to stand up to Mr. Grant. In one episode when Mr. Grant tells Mary he'd like her to hire a new receptionist with a nice "caboose," she's got the perfect retort: "If that is the case, Mr. Grant, why have I been wasting my time for the last two days screening them for skills? I mean why don't I just march them in here in bathing suits?" Mr. Grant gives that a moment's thought. *Hmmm. Maybe not a bad idea*, you can see him thinking. Then he backs down. Mary called him out. Take *that*, Mad Men!

It's hard to believe it, but at the time, this was seen as progressive. In the United States of the 1970s, the office was still a man's world. So when Mr. Grant asks Mary to fix him a drink, she grumbles, but she does it anyway. At least she grumbles about it! As the seasons pass, Mary extends boundaries as an independent career woman—and learns to push back at her boss and call him out on his sexist behavior.

After Lou's wife asks for a separation, he heads to the local pub to drown his sorrows with his coworkers, including Mary. He expects sympathy when he complains about his wife's plan to go back to college. "I'd like to propose a toast to men's lib. Let's hang on to what we got," Lou says.

But Mary isn't having any of it. "Hold it. I can't drink to that," she says. "You invited me so you could hear a woman's point of view. I have been sitting here like some kind of idiot, acting like I agree with everything you said. But I don't agree with everything you've said. As a matter of fact, I don't agree with anything you've said." When Lou accuses her of being on "their side," Mary is furious. "Sides? Oh, Mr. Grant, that is just dumb." There's no need for name-calling, but Mary nails it here—and Mr. Grant respects her because of it.

LIFE LESSON:

Be a Force for Good

Though she's hardly a radical feminist, Mary Richards tries to use her relatively privileged position to help others—and isn't afraid to speak out when she sees injustice or to stand up for her beliefs. In the third season premiere, Mary takes on the issue of pay equity, which was a hot-button issue at the time (and continues to be). When Mary discovers she makes less money than the man who had her job before her, she confronts Lou, albeit in a quavering voice. "I would like to know why the last associate producer before me made fifty dollars a week more than I do."

He doesn't hesitate. "Oh, because he was a man."

She's flustered and momentarily thrown by his blunt response, but then she tells him, "I'm doing as good a job as he did, and I'm getting paid less than he was."

Mr. Grant agrees. In fact, he says she's doing a better job than the guy before her did. Mr. Grant delivers what he thinks is a clever answer: he's got a family and you don't.

But Mary's got an answer for that too. "Mr. Grant, there is no good reason why two people doing the same job at the same place shouldn't be making the same." He gives her a raise, though it's still not as much as the guy who had the job before her got! It doesn't seem like much, but

Mary was at the forefront of change. Compared to her peer group, Mary Richards was doing better than most. In 1970, a newswoman in Mary's position made just 64 percent of what her male colleagues made—and this was actually a higher gender-pay ratio than in most jobs. The average working woman made only 60 percent as much as the average working man at the time.

Another time, Mary's job—and her freedom—is on the line when she refuses to divulge the source for a news story about government kickbacks. In the episode "Will Mary Richards Go to Jail?," Mary Richards does indeed go to jail. Mary, being Mary, makes friends with the prostitutes in her cell. "What are you in here for?" one of them asks. "Imitating a Barbie doll?" When one of her cellmates gets out of jail, Mary even tries to find her legitimate work. Best of all, when she finally goes to court, albeit with a lecherous lawyer who hits on her, the judge dismisses the case and praises Mary as "one of the most charming and competent newsmen that I have ever met." Go Mary!

In another episode, Mary tries to advance the cause of women in broadcasting (and sports) by hiring a female sportscaster, a former (fictitious) Olympic swimmer, Betty Jean Smathers. "I think I may just have had what could be a truly great idea . . . Wouldn't she be fantastic on the news?"

The men in the newsroom don't think the idea is so fantastic. Ted hates the idea. Murray says, "I am not too thrilled by the idea of having my copy mangled by some dummy in a tank suit." Mary tells him she expected this sort of response from Ted but not from him. Isn't he supposed to be the sensitive guy? "I just don't think we gain anything by sticking some pretty little ninny on the news," Murray tells her.

She's not having any of it. "Pretty little ninny? . . . She's bright. She's articulate. She's a woman! That's why you're both against the idea . . . Well, I'm producer of the news, and I think it's a good idea. So that's that."

Well, not quite. When she tells Mr. Grant the idea, he dismisses it as just a gimmick. "You think it would be cute to have a woman do the sports." When he calls her idea "dumb," Mary's had enough. "The idea of hiring Barbara Jean Smathers to do sports is not dumb. What's dumb is rejecting the idea because of some stupid prejudice."

Lou ends up telling her it's her decision to make. "You are the producer, Mary." Don't forget it, Mary! She hires Barbara Jean Smathers as the sportscaster, but it turns out she only wants to report on swimming. Even Mary has to agree she's awful and fires her. Mr. Grant tells her, "You proved that a woman deserves to be just as lousy at a job as a man." Well, that's progress!

Gordy the Weatherman: *Though the show tackled the issue of women in the workplace, it was a decidedly white perspective. Throughout its entire run, there was only one black recurring character, Gordy Howard, played by TV writer, actor, and former football player John Amos. At the time (and even now!) it was rare for a black actor to get a nonstereotypical part on a prime-time series. Amos later said he appreciated the subtlety of the role of Gordy, the meteorologist at WJM. The writers had Phyllis, Ted, and even* a WJM executive mistake Gordy for a sportscaster, typically the token role for a black broadcast journalist at the time. The writers turn it into a running joke where everyone tells Gordy, "Great job with the weather!" And Gordy just laughs to himself. "I liked the fact that he was a meteorologist because it implied that the man could think. I loved it! It was going against the grain, and it showed their sensitivity. They capitalized on the stereotypical thinking," said Amos, who left the show in 1973 when he got the starring role of the patriarch on Norman Lear's all-black family sitcom Good Times. After the third season of that show, Lear ended up firing Amos, who had been vocal about his criticisms of the direction the show was heading. But that was good news for Mary and the gang at WJM because that meant Amos could return to the newsroom—at least temporarily. In the final season of the show, the character of Gordy, now a national network anchorman, gets his own special episode where he returns to visit the gang. Soon after, Amos would land the role of a lifetime, playing the adult Kunta Kinte in the groundbreaking television miniseries Roots, based on Alex Haley's book of the same name. Coincidentally, Amos's old WJM newsroom boss, Ed Asner, also appeared in Roots (as the morally conflicted captain of a slave ship), although they never appeared in the same scene.

CHAPTER FIVE:

HOME

"A room. Actually, an entire apartment, but a single large room. There are some—mostly of the working girl variety—who would consider this place a 'great find': ten-foot ceilings, pegged wood floors, a wood-burning fireplace, and, most important, a fantastic ceiling-height corner window."

—*THE MARY TYLER MOORE SHOW* SCRIPT

Who says you need a big apartment to live large? Mary Tyler Moore's fabulous studio apartment is proof that you don't. The high-beamed ceilings and Palladian windows, which lead to a balcony, give it the open, bright, welcoming feeling of a loft space. It's no surprise that Mary and Rhoda argue over it in the first episode. That's an apartment worth fighting for. *Entertainment Weekly* called it "TV's most famous bachelorette pad." Its eclectic, shabby-chic décor manages to be both classic and modern—just like Mary. Perhaps the most notable thing about Mary's stylish studio apartment is that it is hers and hers alone. The wooden *M* on the wall above her typewriter ensures that you don't forget that.

Located on the third floor of a Queen Anne Victorian in Minneapolis, though it was actually shot on a soundstage in Hollywood, Mary's apartment is part country cottage and part funky crash pad. The shag rug is pure '70s, as are the brown velvet couches, upholstered chairs, and the sunken living room. The french armoire, oak dining set, bay windows, exposed-brick wall, and woodburning Franklin stove add classic touches. She even has a to-die-for walk-in closet leading to a never-seen bathroom. (Perhaps the inspiration for Carrie Bradshaw's walk-in closet on *Sex and the City*?) Unlike most of the picture-perfect artificial homes in other sitcoms of the era, Mary's apartment feels like a real, lived-in room. It's the details that make it believable: the powder-blue phone (rotary dial, of course!) and the wicker furniture.

The apartment is a lot like Mary herself: a blend of old and new, with lots of distinctive touches, like that Toulouse-Lautrec poster and the 1960s space-age lamp by the window. Of course, as with any real apartment, over time, Mary's apartment changes. The set designers reused and reupholstered her furniture and rearranged her knickknacks. One season she's got a baker's rack for her plants. Another season, she's got a wall of built-in bookshelves. But it all feels like home.

LIFE LESSON:

Make the Most of a Small Space

Even though it's a small space, Mary's apartment doesn't seem cluttered. Somehow, it manages to be chock-full of cool things without seeming messy. It's like a ship with a little cubby for everything. To make the most of her small apartment, Mary relies on some time-tested "small-space solutions," including "dual-purpose" or "double-duty" furniture, such as the foldout couch, which turns into her bed. Here are some other small-space tricks that we can borrow from Mary:

- **Take advantage of vertical space:** The tall shelving and hanging pot rack in Mary's kitchen help pack a lot of cookware into a small space. (Granted, she doesn't have to actually stock food or cook in that tiny kitchen.) She's got a paper towel dispenser attached to the underside of her kitchen cabinets to clear counter space (for the spice rack).

- **Create room dividers for privacy:** Mary has a stained glass window in her kitchen, which can be pulled down for private conversations. It's almost like a confessional!

- **Find creative storage solutions:** Mary's got the coolest built-in bookcase built into the raised platform surrounding her sunken living room. There's also built-in shelving beneath the pass-through to the kitchen.

- **Set aside a landing pad:** A landing pad is a space—sometimes a rack or a desk or a shelf—where you can drop your keys and wallet (or phone, nowadays) when you land at home. That way you'll know where they are when you're ready to take off. Mary's landing pad is a handy shelf right next to the door, just where it should be for maximum usage. At one point, Mary has a freestanding wooden coatrack.

Rhoda's attic apartment is microscopic compared to Mary's place, which is saying something considering Mary lives in a studio! No wonder Rhoda is so eager to claim the apartment before Mary does. Like Mary's place, Rhoda's apartment has a distinctive, eclectic style but with a décor that's as artsy and bohemian as Rhoda herself. With its hot-pink walls, fringe lampshade, psychedelic wall art, and a beaded curtain where a door should be, Rhoda's studio apartment is one part hippie and one part pigsty. Instead of a closet, she uses a clothing rack. Rather than a foldout sofa bed like Mary's, Rhoda sleeps on her couch. In fact, her couch is the only place to sleep, or sit, in her apartment, aside from the nearly carnivorous beanbag chair. When Rhoda's mother sits in it, it nearly devours her. Speaking of eating, there's nowhere to eat at Rhoda's place. Her "kitchen" consists of a hot pot and minifridge. Then again, she's always on a diet and seems to live on cottage cheese.

LIFE LESSON:
You Can Entertain in a Small Space

Just because you live in a small apartment doesn't mean you can't entertain, though it will create some unique challenges. Mary manages to host a slew of parties in her studio apartment. The parties themselves are always disastrous, but that has nothing to do with the size of her apartment! It's a testament to Mary's optimism that she continues to throw parties—and a tribute to how much her friends appreciate her that they continue to show up. No doubt, there's also an element of curiosity since everyone wants to see what will go wrong! For instance, consider the time Mary invites a congresswoman to dinner. Sue Ann swoops in to help her but, as usual, only makes things worse. The guests are due at eight o'clock, but Sue Ann insists her prized veal Prince Orloff must be served at exactly eight o'clock: "If we

Mary and Rhoda, Fashion Plates

From the day she strolled into the WJM-TV newsroom in white
go-go boots, a pleated miniskirt, and a low-slung belt, Mary
Richards became a style icon for women around the country,
especially as they entered the workplace en masse. In the decade
before women donned '80s power suits with padded shoulders,
Mary invented her own office style that managed to be both
feminine and professional. As the show progressed and Mary took
on more responsibility in the newsroom, her style matured too.
She knew how to dress for success! She traded in her go-go boots
and miniskirts for tailored blazers, ribbed turtlenecks, pleated
A-line skirts, knit dresses, and bold-colored pantsuits. Designers
such as Marc Jacobs, Isaac Mizrahi, Zac Posen, Tory Burch, and
Michael Kors have singled Mary Richards out as one of the best-
dressed characters in the history of television, as well as a source of
inspiration. "She showed us all what a modern woman looked like—
smart, talented, funny, stylish at work and at home," Michael Kors
said after Mary Tyler Moore's death in 2017. "When I was growing
up, there was nobody else like her."

Leslie Hall, the costume designer for *The Mary Tyler Moore
Show*, had previously designed costumes for *Get Smart* and
would supervise other MTM shows such as *Lou Grant* and
Newhart. It was important for Hall that she keep Mary's working-
woman wardrobe realistic and affordable. She made a deal
with the fashion company Evan-Picone to dress Mary Richards.

The idea was that it would enable Mary to mix, match, and reuse the same items, just as any working woman would. The fact viewers would see Mary rewear the same clothes made her even more relatable.

"The greatest thing that we got from her was a kind of American democratic ideal. Her character represented something that every woman could achieve, whether through her life choices or just through her wardrobe, and we hadn't quite seen that on television before," fashion designer Isaac Mizrahi told *W* magazine after Moore's death. In particular, Mizrahi appreciated that the character managed to be stylish on a budget. "It was TV realism," he said. "You could tell that the character knew how to shop. It wasn't about finding bargains or wholesale clothes. She picked out five or six available dresses and two or three smart pantsuits every season and wore them continuously."

Rhoda's style is equally distinctive but radically different than Mary's, much like their personalities. Even in fashion, Rhoda is the perfect foil for Mary. While Mary's look is neat and fitted, Rhoda's is free-spirited and artsy. She starts out the series wearing oversized, flowy clothing that establishes her as the overweight friend.

Eventually, her character adopts a more bohemian-chic look. Rhoda's forte is her ability to accessorize—with handcrafted bags, chunky necklaces, hoop earrings, and, of course, her signature head scarf. In her memoir, *I, Rhoda*, the late Valerie Harper wrote, "Rhoda's gypsy-woman look became an intrinsic part of her quirky character."

don't eat at eight o'clock, we might as well take my delicious dinner and flush it down the toilet," she says. "Mary, dear, do you have any idea what happens if you let veal Prince Orloff stay in the oven for too long? He dies."

Well, okay then. Let's eat. One more problem: there are exactly six servings of veal, and Lou's got a big appetite—he took three servings!— and Rhoda brought along a surprise guest, Steve Waldman (a young Henry Winkler), a coworker who was just fired. Mary pulls Mr. Grant aside to explain the situation. There's only enough for six people, and he took three servings. "Say, you know what, I'm not as hungry as I thought I was," Mr. Grant says as he scoops up the extra food on his plate and plops it back in the serving dish. Being polite, the congresswoman pretends not to notice. Well, Sue Ann had promised that the dinner would be "a feast to remember." And it certainly is!

Mary can't say that Lou didn't warn her. He was reluctant to come to the dinner party in the first place, telling Mary, "You give rotten parties. It's not that I don't have a good time at your parties, Mary. I've had some of the worst times in my life. Agony. My wife and I broke up at one of your parties, you remember? Not that I'm holding your party responsible, you understand, but it certainly didn't help." He's got a point. Everything that can go wrong does at Mary's parties: Ted and Georgette get into a fight and stop speaking, Murray gets sick, there's a blackout, or Georgette gives birth! Still, Mary doesn't let her small apartment prevent her from entertaining (unfortunately).

LIFE LESSON:
Moving Isn't Easy,
but It's Sometimes Good for You

By season 6, Mary's in a rut. Rhoda has moved back to New York, where she's married on her spin-off show *Rhoda*, and Phyllis has left for San Francisco (and her spin-off show *Phyllis*). Mary gets a letter from Phyllis saying she went swimming with a bunch of seals, got a new job, and is making new friends. Our regularly chipper Mary is feeling down. She's got nothing exciting to report back to Phyllis. "She's dying to find out what's new with me," Mary tells Georgette. "Gee, how depressing. It was bad enough with just Rhoda. Now I've got two friends telling me about their new lives, their new jobs, new friends."

Georgette states what the producers were probably thinking at the time: "This house sure seems empty without Rhoda and Phyllis here." Mary starts to feel like maybe she needs a change of her own. It's been six whole years since she moved to Minneapolis. To mix things up a little, she dyes her hair blonde. But that doesn't seem to work. Sue Ann helps Mary redecorate her apartment, but Mary soon realizes that "it's not my furniture that needs rearranging. It's my life." She contemplates getting a new job, but she loves her job at the newsroom. So instead, she decides to move to a new apartment. That's one way to get out of a rut.

Maybe new surroundings will be good for her. Sure, moving's a drag, but it rewires the brain and gives you a new way of looking at things—at least that's what studies show. It's a way of rebooting your life with new surroundings, a new commute to work, and new neighbors. Best of all, as Mary tells the work gang, her new apartment building has a swimming pool and a tennis court. Her cute studio apartment in the charming Victorian definitely didn't have either of those perks. Just like the move to Minneapolis, Mary's move to her high-rise apartment is the next step for a woman making her own way through the world—with the help of her friends.

The move provides a change of scenery for the character. But, in reality, there was another practical reason for the move. The family who lived in the actual house where the producers had shot the exteriors for Mary's apartment in 1970 was tired of fans showing up and asking if Mary was around. In 1973, when the production returned for additional exterior shots, the family draped a huge "Impeach Nixon" sign over the front of the house. (This was during Watergate.) The producers got the message. Mary would move.

The show's updated opening would feature the outside of Mary's new apartment building instead of the house at 2104 Kenwood Parkway in Minneapolis. Still, that didn't stop the fans from coming. In 1988, when a couple bought the famous television house, they had never seen an episode of the show before and didn't understand the significance. They had some regrets about buying the house once they were facing sometimes as many as thirty tour buses a day to see "where Mary lived." Even fifty years later, fans continue to show up to pay tribute to the house that Mary made famous. The actual house, a single-family home with nine bedrooms and nine bathrooms in 9,500 feet of living space—no problem entertaining there!—sold for around $1.5 million.

Fans don't remember Mary's new apartment as fondly or as vividly—and who can blame them? She doesn't live there nearly as long, and let's face it, it's not as cool as her old place. Sure, she's got a fireplace and a balcony, but it lacks the character of her old bachelorette pad in the Victorian house. No walk-in closet or sunken living room or galley kitchen with stained glass window divider. More importantly, it doesn't have Rhoda or Phyllis. One thing it does have: a bedroom. "Yes, I have my very own bedroom! You don't know how tired I was getting of opening and closing that convertible sofa. Now I've got my own bedroom. It's so exciting," she tells Ted and Georgette and Lou and Sue Ann when they stop by to see the new place. ("Just wait 'til you get a bed!" Sue Ann jokes.) Before heading to dinner, Mary sends her friends ahead so she can have a moment to herself in her new place. She's got something she needs to do on her own. She hangs her iconic wooden *M* on the wall in her new kitchen, marking her new territory.

Later that night, after dinner, they return to her apartment, which is completely unfurnished. But that doesn't stop them from celebrating. They sit on the carpeting and drink champagne out of plastic cups. Mary's feeling sentimental. "I guess it's only natural to move into a new place and feel that way about your old place. I remember I felt that way about my old place when I moved from my old old place. But with all you guys here, it's beginning to feel like home already!"

That's another good life lesson: home is where your friends and family are. And just like that, Mary's out of her rut and back to being her usual cheery self.

CHAPTER SIX:
FEMINISM

"Girls are always supposed to get little girl toys, dolls, play stoves, little dishes, it's all part of the plot to launch them into their little roles as housewives."

—PHYLLIS LINDSTROM

The show was a reflection of the times, in which women were pushing for change in visible, public ways, and the media was taking note—because they had no other choice. In the spring of 1970, just six months before the show's premiere, a group of one hundred feminists staged a sit-in at the offices of *Ladies Home Journal* to push for more positive female representation in media. When *Newsweek* published "Women in Revolt," a cover story on the burgeoning women's liberation movement, forty-six women on staff filed a gender discrimination suit against the news magazine—and won! The kicker was that the newsweekly had had to hire an outside woman to write the story because they hadn't promoted the women working there.

In August 1970, just one month before *The Mary Tyler Moore Show* went on the air, fifty thousand feminists paraded down New York City's Fifth Avenue as part of the Women's Strike for Equality March. Sponsored by the National Organization for Women (NOW), it was the brainchild of Betty Friedan, author of the 1963 bestseller *The Feminine Mystique*. The groundbreaking book challenged the notion that a woman's role in society is to be a housewife and is credited with kickstarting the second-wave feminist movement, a.k.a. women's liberation (or the catchier *women's lib*). The first-wave feminist movement was primarily concerned with basic freedoms for women, such as the right to vote. After women achieved the right to vote, the second wave pushed for equal legal and social rights, including equal opportunity in employment and education. And into that very heightened moment, Mary Richards, a single working woman, arrived in prime time, providing a new role model for independent young women.

While Mary Tyler Moore herself never identified as a feminist, the character of Mary Richards might have done more for the women's lib movement than any other fictitious character. Mary was a spunky professional woman, more focused on work and friends than on marriage, and in that way, she broke the mold of what a woman should be. Who says you need a man and children to lead a happy life? The show was never vocally politically minded in the way that, say, *All in the Family*, which went on the air six months later, was. It took on feminist issues—such as birth control, sex discrimination, reproductive rights, and pay equity—but it never took them on with a shout. Mary let us know her mind in her own quiet way. Mary Richards "was a woman who stood up for herself whenever she spotted inequity but who wasn't going to push it to the edge. She made little squeaks and noises and was among the first to do so," Moore later said.

LIFE LESSON:
Push for Change
(Even If It's Just a Gentle Push)

So Mary isn't a radical, but her mere existence in the newsroom is pretty radical. Like real women joining fields that had previously only been open to men, Mary is often in the position of being the designated representative female. "It used to be I felt I could be myself. Now I feel I represent women everywhere," Mary gripes to Rhoda as she prepares for a meeting at the station. She resents how the new station manager is always "trotting in groups of people and saying, 'This is our woman executive!'" Mary supports women's causes but not in a strident way. She doesn't declare she's prochoice, but she makes it clear that she supports a woman's right to make reproductive choices. Murray pressures his wife to have another child even though they have three girls. As Lou, the self-described male chauvinist pig, explains, "A man doesn't feel complete until he has a son."

Mary responds, "I don't think it's fair to ask Marie to have a baby if she doesn't want one." Okay, she's not exactly walking in a prochoice march, but in her own way, Mary is supporting women's rights.

You could applaud her for pushing for change, or you could just as easily criticize her for being a pushover. Gloria Steinem and some other feminist activists and critics complained she was too wishy-washy and not vocal enough. Mary twists herself into contortions not to hurt any-one's feelings, and she's not exactly a go-getter. At one point, Lou tells her, "We got this memo from personnel about how to treat women different and don't give them those crummy little jobs like women are sup-posed to do."

Mary meekly replies, "I don't mind making your coffee."

"You don't agree with that memo, do you?" he asks.

"Well, I sort of suggested it." It's played for laughs, but it says a lot about Mary's apologetic nature in the office. Though she never marries over the course of the show, some critics have pointed out that she is the "de facto wife and mother of her office family."

Then there's the time that Lou is promoted to the executive suite, and Mary outright tells him she doesn't want to be considered as his replacement. She tells Phyllis and Rhoda, "I don't think I'd do a rotten job and get myself fired. I just don't know if being the head of a newsroom is a woman's job."

Luckily, Phyllis sets her straight: "There you go, 'woman's job,' 'man's job.' There's no such thing. Name one job that a man can handle that a woman can't." Phyllis encourages Mary to take the job, not just for herself but for womankind. "This isn't just you reaching for the next plateau; it's *us*." Phyllis eventually changes Mary's mind, and she marches into Mr. Grant's office to tell him she's had second thoughts about the job. But he says she wasn't even a contender.

MARY: Mr. Grant, why wasn't I a great choice? Does it have anything to do with my ability?

MR. GRANT: No! Are you kidding?

MARY: It's not because I'm a woman, is it?

MR. GRANT: Of course it is.

What can you say to this kind of blatant sexism? Mary's eyes narrow, and she glares at Mr. Grant. She silently marches out of his office and never mentions it again.

As the series went on and feminist attitudes became more accepted, TV critics took the show's writers to task for not giving Mary more important work to do in the newsroom. Feminists noticed that the theme song calls Mary a girl even though she's clearly a woman. A *New York Times* critic complained that Mary "hardly ever gets to write the news or report it on camera—even though she appears to be several times brighter than the men who do." Still, compared to the female characters on TV at the time, Mary was down-right radical. Shows like *Bewitched* and *I Dream of Jeannie* involved scenarios where a woman has special powers, but the man in her life won't let her use them!

Mary had made it out of the kitchen and into the office, but for some feminists, she didn't go far enough. Groundbreaking feminist Shirley Chisholm, the first African American woman in Congress (1968), was a fan of the show . . . sort of. In 1977, when the show was about to go off the air, Chisholm told *Esquire* magazine, "One of the delightful aspects of the show is that it has featured a single woman making it in a male-dominated occupation. But why does Mary always call her boss 'Mr. Grant,' while her male colleagues refer to him as 'Lou'?" A real-life Mary Richards loved the show: Barbara Walters. Walters, who in 1974 became cohost of the NBC News morning program *The Today Show*, the first woman to hold the position on an American news program, felt it accurately reflected the newsroom gender dynamics. "What Mary Richards goes through with Lou, that kind of apology before blurting things out—there's nothing-personal, it's-not-something-I'm-asking-for-myself—every woman in the industry still goes through that," Walters told *Esquire*. "It's just a marvelously funny program, and essentially what makes it so is the charm and the humor and the straightforwardness of Mary Tyler Moore. Someday I hope Mary Richards gets my job."

When Mary Tyler Moore died in 2017, *Newsweek* wrote, "It would be an understatement to say *The Mary Tyler Moore Show* was an important moment in the women's rights movement in the 1970s. Mary Richards—single, living alone, forging her own career—was an example for many women of the era. The fact that she was played by Moore, who was then known for being Dick Van Dyke's better half on TV, made it an even bigger statement. In many ways, Moore playing Richards represented countless other women who, once defined by the man they were with, were now free to make it on their own."

From June Cleaver to Mary Richards

In the 1950s, women's roles on TV sitcoms were generally limited to traditional housewives such as June Cleaver. In *The Honeymooners*, Ralph often threatened his wife with violence—"To the moon, Alice!"—and Lucy's show biz ambitions on *I Love Lucy* often got her in trouble with her husband, Ricky Ricardo, who would bellow, "Lucy, you've got some 'splaining to do!" By the 1960s, women in prime-time series were either married or widowed. A new slew of shows were at least depicting women striving for independence. Granted, they were mostly monsters or witches. Samantha, the witchy housewife on *Bewitched*, had more power than her husband, Darrin, but his male ego was too threatened to allow her to use it. On *I Dream of Jeannie,* despite being the title character, Jeannie (Barbara Eden) is submissive to her master and uses her power mostly to please him (and even then, it backfires!). Symbolic or what?

That Girl, which premiered in 1966, four years before *The Mary Tyler Moore Show*, introduced audiences to the idea of a single woman living on her own in the big city. In that show, Marlo Thomas, daughter of comedian Danny Thomas (*Make Room for Daddy*), plays Ann Marie, an aspiring actress who moves to New York for her big show business break. She's on her own but hardly alone. Her overprotective father is always hovering around, worried about his ditzy daughter, and she soon falls in love with magazine executive Donald Hollinger. By the fifth season, she is engaged to Donald (played by the actor Ted Bessell, who later appears on *The Mary Tyler Moore Show* as one of Mary's steady boyfriends, Joe Warner).

After five seasons, the show's producers were pushing for Thomas to marry Donald, but Thomas refused. She didn't want it to seem as if marriage had been Ann Marie's goal from the beginning. As Thomas said later, "We opened up the window for young women. You did not have to be the wife or the daughter of somebody or the secretary of somebody, but that you could be the somebody. The story could be about you and what you wanted in life. Once that happened, I think that really paved the way for a lot of other shows." In fact, James Brooks, the cocreator of *The Mary Tyler Moore Show*, had honed his craft as a writer for *That Girl*.

Julia, which aired from 1968 to 1971, took things even further: it was the first sitcom to revolve around a single African American professional woman. Played by actress Diahann Carroll, Julia is a widowed single mother who works as a nurse in a doctor's office at a large aerospace company. It was the first prime-time show to feature an African American woman as a lead character rather than as a servant. Though it was groundbreaking in that way, critics complained it was apolitical and didn't represent the realities of what it was like to be black in America—especially in the turbulent late '60s. Besides, what single, black working mother of a young child could afford a sumptuous apartment and a glamorous wardrobe like Julia's? But whoever said sitcoms were realistic? Even

Carroll called the show "a fantasy," explaining that's how it was acceptable in prime time: "I'm a black woman with a white image. I'm as close as they can get to have the best of both worlds. The audience can accept me for the same reason: I don't scare them." For her, just having an independent black professional woman in prime time was a start. "There was nothing like this young successful mother on the air, and we thought that it might be a very good stepping stone," said Carroll. It was a stepping-stone leading the way for Mary Tyler Moore and other single professional women in prime time.

MTM Trivia: *Who's that woman? When Mary Richards tosses her hat in the opening credits for the show, an old woman with a kerchief on her head seems to lurk in the background. She appears to be scowling at Mary. That iconic moment continues to be popular with millennial fans, who have turned the image into many a gif. Nobody knew the woman's name, Hazel Frederick, until she introduced herself to Moore at a book signing for Moore's autobiography,* After All, *in 1996. It turned out that the seemingly grouchy woman wasn't disapproving at all. She hadn't seen the cameras filming Moore and was mostly concerned for the woman who seemed to be running into traffic in one of the city's busiest intersections. Or as Moore put it, "She just thought there was a lunatic about to lose her life." Later, Moore said that Frederick was right to be worried: "I'm really lucky that I came out of that alive." Regardless of what Frederick was really thinking, her prudish scowl in the background came to represent the past, our parents, and authority. Heck, she was old age, and Mary was youth, future, and opportunity.*

LIFE LESSON:

Honor Those Who Paved Your Way

Perhaps as a response to critics who complained about some of the show's negative stereotypes of women (ditzy Georgette or "desperate for male attention" Sue Ann), in the sixth season, the writers introduced a new strong female guest star. Played by Academy Award–winning actress Eileen Heckart, Flo Meredith, Mary's aunt (well, actually second cousin, but they're close), is a globe-trotting, name-dropping journalist who can drink Lou under the table. (She orders "scotch on the rocks, easy on the rocks.") Dressed in a black suit with a black hat to go with it, Aunt Flo shows up in Minneapolis looking like she means business. In fact, she's in town on business—she's covering a murder trial and has managed to nab an exclusive interview with the accused. Mary is in awe of Aunt Flo, saying, "She has the most fantastic life, gets exclusive interviews with the greatest celebrities."

Aunt Flo is also more than a little bit patronizing when she refers to the newsroom as "a cute little place," which rubs macho Mr. Grant the wrong way. "It's not all that little, and it's not all that cute," he says grumpily. To make it worse, she tells Lou and Mary how they should be devoting more time to the murder trial and less time to the local news. She boasts about how she has won sixteen journalistic awards, and she supposedly slept with Winston Churchill. It's hard to compete with that. Mary is very impressed and more than a little bit intimidated.

Later Mary gushes to Murray, "She's incredible. She's the most dynamic person I've ever met." But she's also annoyed at Aunt Flo's prickly attitude and the fact she's a blowhard.

Flo keeps topping Lou's career highlights, recounting story after story of her wild adventures, like the time she almost got killed collecting evidence that landed her a scoop and a corrupt commissioner in prison: "I had to crawl a mile through a sewer pipe to escape. But it was worth it," she says, later adding that "life is too short to get stuck behind a desk." Next to polite Mary, who asks permission for more responsibility, Aunt Flo is an unapologetic badass.

"How could you do that? You kept topping him on everything he said," Mary complains to Aunt Flo after she insults Mr. Grant.

Mary apologizes to Lou the next day, saying, "I'm really sorry about what happened last night. I mean the way my aunt treated you."

Mary gripes to Mr. Grant about how her aunt is sometimes hard to handle. Mr. Grant, of all people, gives credit to the first wave of feminists, including Aunt Flo. "You see, Mary, when your aunt started out, she was a pioneer. All working women were. Pioneers have to be tough. They don't win popularity contests. People like Flo Meredith broke the ground for people like Mary Richards."

Mary smiles broadly. "Boy, you know something. Sometimes you really surprise me. You're not what I'd call a liberated man, but sometimes, Mr. Grant . . . wow."

Another surprise for Mary: she finds out that Flo and Lou went bar-hopping together and danced the tango. "Next time I'm in Minneapolis, maybe we can finish up where we left off," Aunt Flo tells Lou as she prepares to say goodbye. Then she takes Lou's face in her hands and plants a big wet smacker on his lips.

Mary's jaw hits the floor. "You're going to finish up where you left off?" She is shocked.

"Hey, if I was good enough for Churchill," says Flo, blowing a kiss to Lou before she leaves.

When Flo returns to Minneapolis, Lou proposes. But she doesn't want to marry him—or anyone. "Why don't we just take the honeymoon and skip the wedding?" asks a disappointed Lou. Flo is having way too much fun globe-trotting and canoodling with world leaders to ever settle down, even with a, uh, catch like Lou. And he's sure not going to put up with a wife who's never home to make his dinner. Yet even this self-styled sexist pig finds his views about a woman's place have been changed by Aunt Flo. And with Lou, maybe a few other minds got changed too out there in TV land. Thanks, Flo!

The episode ends with a laugh as Ted shares his opinion on Aunt Flo, who he deems "unfeminine." He tells Mary, "I have to tell you, your aunt is pushy and arrogant. This goes against nature. Women should be gentle and refined. If God had intended for them to be pushy and arrogant, he'd have made them men."

MTM Trivia: *Betty White, who plays Sue Ann Nivens on the show, was almost cast as man-hungry Blanche on* The Golden Girls, *until director Jay Sandrich told the producers to rethink the casting lest she be stereotyped. "If Betty plays another man-hungry neighborhood you-know-what, they're going to equate it with Sue Ann and think it's just a continuation of that." Instead, Betty White was cast as the naive Rose character and actress Rue McClanahan was cast as Blanche.*

LIFE LESSON:
Love Yourself

Perhaps the most feminist thing you can do as a woman is love yourself. Treva Silverman, the young writer who provided most of the lines for Rhoda, based a lot of the situations and humor on her own experiences. Later, she pointed out that Rhoda's character arc mirrors the experience of many women in the women's liberation movement, including her own. In the first couple of seasons, Rhoda relentlessly puts down her looks and obsesses about finding a man. When Valerie Harper lost weight before season 3, Brooks and Burns saw it as a good opportunity for the character of Rhoda to grow. They figured since the show was character-driven, the story lines should reflect changing characters—and maybe even the evolving characters of the real people who play them. Brooks and Burns asked Silverman to write an episode about Rhoda's weight loss and insecurities since she, too, had struggled with her weight and body image.

She later recalled that writing the episode was an emotional experience for her. "Jim and Allan, knowing that I'd spent my life on and off diets, said, 'We want you to write a show explaining what this twenty pounds means.' I put a lot of my feelings into it. I knew the whole thing of losing weight and gaining weight, what it did to her pride and to her fears. She couldn't be the old knockabout Rhoda anymore. So much of that was extremely moving to me. I remember crying as I wrote the ending, which is hard to do—type and cry, type and cry."

In the episode "Rhoda the Beautiful," Rhoda loses twenty pounds at Calorie Cutters but still can't stop putting herself down. She tells Mary, "All my life, I've had this weight thing. I always thought if I could lose those twenty pounds, I would start to look okay." She can't quite believe that she's lost weight and has a hard time accepting compliments about it.

Even Phyllis is impressed with her weight loss, although she expresses it in a typically indelicate way: "You really dropped a ton." But Rhoda can barely look at herself in the mirror, she's so uncomfortable in her own skin.

Mary stands in front of the mirror with her and tells her, "Forget the Rhoda who does lots of put-downs of herself and just look at yourself like a stranger. I wish you could begin to feel good about the way you look."

But it's not just about the weight—it's about the way that the weight has become a comfortable excuse for her unhappiness. "This is the first time in my life I can't say, 'Boy, if I could just lose twenty pounds, just think how terrific I'd look.'"

By the end of the episode, Rhoda confesses to Mary that she won first place in a beauty pageant at Hemple's Department Store, where she works. At first, she says, she didn't want to tell anyone, because she "was afraid everybody would make jokes." But she realizes it's time to accept that she's beautiful—with or without the extra twenty pounds. She puts on the cheesy cape and crown they gave her and proudly declares, "I won! After thirty-two years, me!" After that episode, Rhoda's character becomes more confident and less focused on her appearance, although she's still desperate for a man!

Just as Rhoda struggles with body image and self-acceptance, so did many of the women who watched. Young women were just starting to break free from traditional expectations, like marriage and motherhood, but there was still so much pressure to look a certain way. Feminists had not yet begun to embrace the idea that fat (or body image) is a feminist issue, and it would be decades before body positivity became a thing. Rhoda and the show were both a reflection of the time and an influence on the time. For her work on this episode, Silverman became the first solo female writer to win an Emmy for comedy writing.

CHAPTER SEVEN:

HUMOR

"Mary, I came to Minneapolis
because of the cold. I figured if I was frozen,
I'd keep better."

—RHODA

It's no wonder that the CBS mustaches didn't know what to make of those early *Mary Tyler Moore Show* scripts. The laughs all came from a different place than they did on other shows. The quick-witted, character-based humor was so unlike any other sitcom on the air at the time. Rather than getting laughs from supernatural situations (*Bewitched, I Dream of Jeannie*) or gimmicky setups (*The Beverly Hillbillies, Green Acres*), *The Mary Tyler Moore Show* drew humor from its quirky characters. The more you got to know the characters, the funnier the show became. As writer Treva Silverman put it, "Each character seems to be talking on a one-to-one basis to somebody in the audience, kind of firsthand, just as if you were talking to your friend and were describing something funny."

Even though she was the star of the show, Mary Tyler Moore never thought of herself as being funny. "My forte is not being funny but reacting in a funny way to those around me," she said. That's partially what inspired the writers to create an ensemble show with all of the comic characters in conflict with each other and Mary playing the straight woman in the middle. Of course, it wouldn't have worked without Mary's outsized ability to fake laughter, her impeccable comic timing, and the priceless facial expressions that conveyed so much more than a punch line ever could. Or, as the show's executive producer James Brooks put it, "If Mary was in a French movie and you didn't speak French, you'd laugh at her."

Another thing that made the show so funny was its ability to surprise audiences with jokes they could never see coming. Just when you thought you knew where a joke was heading, it would spin in an entirely different direction and hit you when and where you least expected it. For example, there's the episode where Phyllis tries to set her bachelor brother, Ben (Robert Moore), up with Mary, only to find that he's more interested in spending time with Rhoda, who seems to enjoy his company. Since Phyllis hates Rhoda, she's horrified by the idea of her perfect brother hooking up with her nemesis. She's miserable at the prospect that they'll have to accept Rhoda as a sister-in-law. Rhoda tries to explain that she's got the wrong idea.

RHODA: Ben and I aren't getting married. He's not my type.

Now Phyllis is even more horrified—who does Rhoda think she is to reject Phyllis's beloved brother?

PHYLLIS: Why? My brother is successful. He's handsome. He's intelligent.

RHODA: He's gay!

PHYLLIS: He's what?

RHODA: He's gay. I thought for sure you knew, Phil. We're not getting married.

Harper recalled later, "The audience didn't see it coming. They roared. The laughter went on so long that Cloris [Leachman, who played Phyllis] and I had to keep on acting silently until she could deliver her rejoinder: 'Oh, Rhoda, I'm *so relieved.*'"

The joke probably wouldn't work today—and some critics have complained that Rhoda casually outs Ben. But at the time, it worked because it was totally unexpected. Nobody had ever uttered the word *gay* to mean homosexual before on television—and certainly not in such an accepting way. Remember the Stonewall Riots had just launched the gay rights movement a few years earlier. There still weren't any out TV or movie characters or stars. Also, for what it's worth, the role of Ben was played by Tony-nominated stage veteran Robert Moore, a gay man who was happy to play one on TV. He loved the fact the joke wasn't at the gay character's expense.

LIFE LESSON:
Find Humor in Tragedy

Face it: life is funny, sometimes in tragic ways—and sometimes the funniest things are the darkest. That was the case in one of the most famous episodes of the show: "Chuckles the Clown," which frequently lands atop lists of best TV episodes of all time. This episode manages to pack in nonstop punch lines that all culminate in a laugh fest—at a funeral.

It begins with Ted excitedly announcing to the newsroom that he's going to be the grand marshal of the circus parade . . . Until Lou, well, rains on his parade.

> **LOU:** Forget it, Ted. You aren't. I said forget it. My TV anchorman isn't marching down the street with a chimp. It will give him an undignified image.
>
> **TED:** Oh, Lou, it won't give me an undignified image.
>
> **LOU:** I was talking about the chimp.

Ted complains to Mary:

TED: After giving seven of the best years I've got, Lou still treats me like dirt. He treats me like a child, Mary.

MARY: Oh, Ted. That's not true. Oh, sure, maybe he bosses you around, but he doesn't treat you like a child. He respects you as a mature adult.

TED: Then why won't he let me go to the circus?

Classic Ted, complaining that he's treated like a child and then acting like one. That's funny!

When Ted learns he's being replaced as grand marshal of the circus parade by Chuckles the Clown, he says, "I hate to say this, but I hope they laugh at him."

So right away, the audience assumes the episode is going to focus on the conflict between Ted and Lou. But things go in a decidedly unexpected direction when Lou stumbles into the office in a daze with some bad news: "Oh Lord, oh dear . . . something terrible has happened. Someone we all know is dead." Murray and Mary are obviously distraught and want to know who died. It takes Lou a moment before saying somberly, "Chuckles the Clown is dead. It was a freak accident. He went to the parade dressed as Peter Peanut, and a rogue elephant tried to shell him."

Lou shares the sad news with Ted, during a commercial break for the six o'clock news, only Ted thinks he's joking. "Stop trying to cheer me up, Lou. That's funny, but that's in bad taste."

But Lou says it's not a joke and Ted's got to present a eulogy for Chuckles on air without any time to prepare. "Don't worry. I won't let you down," Ted says, which we all know means he's about to bomb.

In his deep anchorman voice, Ted's eulogy is decidedly cringeworthy. He shares "The Credo of the Clown," a poem that Chuckles used to recite at the end of each program. "'A little song, a little dance, a little seltzer down your pants.' That's what it's all about, folks. That's what he stood for; that's what gave his life meaning. Chuckles liked to make people laugh," Ted tells viewers. "I'd like to think that somewhere, up there tonight, in his honor, a choir of angels is sitting on whoopee cushions."

The next day at the newsroom, Sue Ann, Murray, and Lou can't stop making jokes about the bizarre circumstances of Chuckles's death. (Can you blame them?)

Murray gets in some good zingers, including, "It could have been worse. He could have gone as Billy Banana and had an elephant peel him to death." When Lou says it's "lucky that elephant didn't go after somebody else," Murray answers, "That's right. After all, you know how hard it is to stop after just one peanut."

Mary is upset about Chuckles's death and disappointed in the way her coworkers—especially Murray—are joking about it. At the funeral, Murray tells a joke about how they'll be able to recognize Chuckles's clown friends because they'll be climbing out of a little hearse. Mary chides him. "This is a funeral. A man has died. We came here to show respect, not to laugh." Murray apologizes and promises there'll be no more jokes.

But as soon as the funeral service begins and the reverend lists off some of the characters Chuckles played over the years, including Billy Banana, Mr. Fe-Fi-Fo, and Aunt Yoohoo, Mary catches a case of the giggles. She contorts her face trying to stifle the laughter; she coughs to try to cover it up, but it's no use. The other funeral guests are looking at her disapprovingly.

The reverend stops his sermon to tell her it's okay to laugh. Chuckles would appreciate it. "He lived to make people laugh. Tears were offensive to him, deeply offensive . . . So go ahead, my dear—laugh for Chuckles," he says. At that moment, Mary breaks down sobbing, which, ironically, is hilarious.

As Lou explains earlier in the episode, laughing at death is "a relief, a kind of defense mechanism. It's like whistling in a graveyard. You laugh at something that scares ya. We laugh at death because we know that death will have the last laugh on us." Like many of the best—and funniest—moments on the show, this episode toggles between humor and pathos, leaving the audience to laugh so hard they cry.

MTM Trivia: *The actor who played Chuckles the Clown in the only episode where he speaks is Richard Schaal, who was married to Valerie Harper at the time. He also played both Paul and Howard Arnell, brothers who date Mary. He went on to have recurring roles on Mary Tyler Moore Show spin-offs* Phyllis *and* Rhoda.

The Mary Tyler Moore Show **Fan Club**

Oprah Winfrey is probably the biggest celebrity fan of *The Mary Tyler Moore Show*—she went so far as to re-create the iconic set from the show on *Oprah*. Among other luminaries who point to the show as an inspiration: TV powerhouses such as Tina Fey, Amy Poehler, Ray Romano, Lena Dunham, Lena Waithe, Jim Parsons, and Shonda Rhimes.

Here are some of the things they've said about the show and what it means to them:

"The show was a light in my life, and Mary was a trailblazer for my generation. She's the reason I wanted my own production company . . . I was sixteen years old when I first saw this groundbreaking show. I watched this show every Saturday night like my life depended on it. I wanted to walk through those doors and sit at Mary's desk."—**Oprah Winfrey**

"I watched *The Mary Tyler Moore Show* all the time and fantasized that I was Rhoda. I wanted to be Mary's best friend. Her being able to play humiliation as well as she did was very appealing."—**Julia Louis-Dreyfus (*Seinfeld*, *Veep*)**

"It was a sitcom, which could be big and broad, but there was something so real about her (Mary Tyler Moore). When we did our show, that was one of the shows we tried to emulate, you know? That kind of style."—**Ray Romano (*Everybody Loves Raymond*)**

"I was obsessed with *The Mary Tyler Moore Show*."—**Lena Waithe** (*The Chi, Master of None*), who has said she wants to make a Mary Tyler Moore biopic.

"There was a night of TV that was '*Mary Tyler Moore*' and that was a sacred night for me. That show was a big, big deal."—**Tina Fey** (*30 Rock*)

Former First Lady Michelle Obama is also a fan:

"At no point did the series end in a happy ending with her finding a husband—which seemed to be the course you had to take as a woman . . . I was probably ten or eleven when I saw that, and sort of started thinking . . . having a family is an option. And going to school and getting your education and building your career is another viable option that can lead to happiness and fulfillment." —**Michelle Obama**

Here's what some celebrities had to say about the show back in 1977 when it went off the air:

"*The Mary Tyler Moore Show* is the only network show I consistently watch, aside from the news and *Sesame Street*. She seems at once positive, vivacious, vulnerable, attractive, independent, adventurous, and feminine."—**Robert Redford**

"*The Mary Tyler Moore Show* is one of the oases in what has been called the wasteland of television."—**Alfred Hitchcock**

"Before *The Mary Tyler Moore Show*, I don't believe there had ever been a woman living alone and having affairs—being independent. I think Mary had considerable influence on the character of Mary Richards, too—for example the episode where she demands equal pay. Ultimately there was a 'TV solution'—she gets only half the difference."—**Gloria Steinem**

"It's my favorite program—there's nobody like Mary Tyler Moore. She's fresh without being icky-poo. And there's enough reality to all of the characters to make them believable to those of us in the business. I think one roots for all of them. In his own way, each one of them is a loser who somehow comes out ahead."—**Barbara Walters**

"It's really one of my favorite TV shows, especially because of its great spin-offs. I've been following Mary's career since *The Dick Van Dyke Show*."—**Andy Warhol**

"*The Mary Tyler Moore Show* was the first modern situation comedy in which the female star was not only not married but not engaged—but the important thing was that Mary Richards didn't even seem to care. There she was, turning the world on with her smile in the opening montage of the show, walking along with a bagful of groceries in her arms, and you could tell that she was on her way home to cook herself dinner for one."—**Nora Ephron**

LIFE LESSON:
Use Humor to Deal with an Awkward Situation

As Chuckles's funeral shows, humor often helps us cope during stressful times. It also comes in handy when trying to defuse an awkward or embarrassing situation, which describes so many moments during *The Mary Tyler Moore Show*. Ted is the dolt who always manages to say the awkward thing that everyone else is thinking but is too tactful to say. His character is too clueless and self-involved to realize how stupid/funny his comments are, but he still makes everyone laugh. (Granted, they're often laughing at him, not with him.)

When Mary brings Ken, a single dad she's dating, to the office after lunch, Ted pronounces (in front of Ken) "just because his first marriage didn't work out doesn't mean he's gonna botch it again." He thinks he's being helpful and insightful, which makes it funnier.

After Ken leaves, Mary sets Ted straight:

MARY: Ted, do you trust me?

TED: Sure, I trust you, Mary.

MARY: Would you take off your left shoe?

TED: Okay.

MARY: Now would you take off your sock?

TED: Yes.

MARY: Listen very carefully. The next time you see me talking to somebody and you think of something to say that would be appropriate or add to the conversation, I want you to take that sock and stuff it down your throat.

TED: What about the shoe?

Again, it's funny because we don't expect it. In fact, it's totally unexpected and against type for Mary, who is usually so nice and direct. Here she's just direct. If Lou said that to Ted, it would just be plain mean. Here it's funny. And then it's even funnier because—classic Ted—he doesn't understand the joke at all. Remember—Ted's the guy who reads his stage directions out loud on the air (i.e., "take off glasses and look serious"), thinks Albania is the capital of New York state, and accidentally leaves his makeup bib on while he delivers the news.

In one episode, Lou explains Ted's appeal: "I guess he's not the world's worst anchorman. He's no Walter Cronkite, no John Chancellor, no Harry Reasoner. But he's got something that they don't have—*unpredictability*. Oh sure, you know when you watch him that he's going to put his foot in his mouth. But the thing you can never figure out is, how is he going to get the *other* one in there with it?"

LIFE LESSON:
It's Okay to Laugh at Yourself

So much of the show's humor comes from the characters we know so well but who still manage to surprise us. For instance, Mary is a pretty, straitlaced good girl and often jokes about it. When Sherry, her old cell-mate, a prostitute, designs a cutout dress that leaves little to the imagination, Mary explains why she doesn't want to try it on: "I'm just a little old fashioned, modest. When we were kids, we used to play doctor. I used to play the receptionist." This is the same Mary who half-jokes, "Once I went into a bookstore to buy a copy of *Everything You Wanted to Know About Sex* (*But Were Afraid to Ask)*. I was afraid to ask for the book."

But every once in a while, Mary surprises us with an edgy comment that might not strike us as funny if it had come from, say, bawdy Sue Ann. In "Phyllis Whips Inflation," Phyllis needs to find a job after her husband cuts off her credit cards (gasp!). The only problem is she doesn't have any marketable skills. "He actually had the temerity to suggest that I start living within a budget. What does he expect? That I'm going to write down every one hundred dollars I spend?" Phyllis is furious about it. She explains: "To me, spending money is part of living beautiful. It's an art. Maybe there are some people who can live within the restrictions of a budget, but for me, it would be like trying to make love in a straitjacket."

To which our sweet, innocent Mary replies, "Hey, don't knock it 'til you've tried it." Phyllis looks shocked. Again, it sounds like something Sue Ann would say. Coming from Mary, it's unexpected and hilarious.

Each character specializes in a different type of humor. Sue Ann's best jokes rely on double entendres and sexual innuendos. She's always got sex on the brain, like when Lou and Murray are laughing about

Chuckles's bizarre death, and Sue Ann says, "I don't know what you two are laughing about, but I'll take a chance, it's dirty."

Sue Ann and Mary have a subtle competition going—or at least Sue Ann does. She's threatened by the fact Mary is a fellow single woman and she's younger and more attractive to men. Sue Ann likes to tease Mary about her relative sexual inexperience. "Doesn't it ever bother you that you were the obvious favorite of a group of men who spend their time with dead people?" she asks Mary at a morticians' convention.

When Georgette goes into labor at one of Mary's awful parties, Murray announces, "A woman is giving birth to a baby in Mary's bedroom."

Sue Ann responds, "I know! And it's probably the most exciting thing that will ever happen in there!"

Lou and Murray's jokes are usually about Ted (who can blame them?). When Ted boasts, "I even got cheered for cutting a ribbon at a supermarket!" Murray has the perfect comeback: "That's because they didn't think you could do it."

Rhoda uses put-down humor . . . to put down herself. Again, sometimes it's healthy to laugh at yourself. She jokes, "When we used to play Mommy and Daddy when I was a kid, I always played Mommy's unmarried sister." Rhoda seems to have an endless stream of one-liners: "Life insurance, huh? I still haven't met a beneficiary."

As Harper explained in her memoir, *I, Rhoda*, Rhoda "was written for anyone who used humor to hide struggle, sadness, and fear. Anyone who wanted someone to commiserate with over body-image issues and boy trouble could turn to Rhoda. Anyone who dreamed big and fell flat had a friend in Rhoda. And then anyone who kept going had her as an ally."

There's something funny about acknowledging your own quirks and being able to laugh at them. Ted is the only character who never seems to laugh at himself—because he never gets the jokes!

CHAPTER EIGHT

KINDNESS

Mary: Mr. Grant, you're gonna be just fine, just fine. Go in there and be natural. And remember to smile.

Lou: You can't have both things, Mary.

—FROM "THOROUGHLY UNMILITANT MARY"

Humor and kindness don't usually mix well, except on *The Mary Tyler Moore Show*. Mary Richards leads by example and shows that you can be a dynamic, independent professional woman and still be a total sweetheart. James Brooks said, "Mary believed that people should be open and loving toward one another." Mary's kind nature acts as a foil for the other characters—and she gently nudges them to become better people. The other characters are constantly cutting each other down, but with Mary's help, they occasionally manage to put aside their sniping and help one another. This peacemaking is a major theme of the show. Everyone's got some redeeming features, and even idiots like Ted Baxter deserve some respect. You could say that Ted's daily "Hi, guys!" as he enters the office is its own form of kindness.

Studies have shown that kindness—even in small doses—is actually good for your health. An Oxford University study showed that being kind results in a "substantial and measurable effect" on well-being. Or, as the study's lead author, Dr. Oliver Scott Curry, put it, "Performing acts of kindness will not change your life, but might help nudge it in the right direction." That's certainly the case in the WJM newsroom.

Of course, there are many different ways to show kindness, and some are more obvious than others. Just holding the door open for someone, complimenting them, or smiling at someone can be an act of kindness. Forgiving someone, showing respect, and being generous without expecting anything in return are all ways to show kindness.

Sometimes just taking the time to find out why a friend is down or taking a coworker out to lunch is the best way to be kind. Mary showers kindness on her friends and coworkers: complimenting them, lending them clothing, and advising them on their love lives and careers. However, rather than being sappy, Mary's kindness generates many gags—like the time she discovers that Murray is a compulsive gambler, and she tries to rescue him from a poker game with the newsroom guys. It's a serious topic, but it's impossible not to laugh since the game is taking place in "Artie's Castle," a fake castle set for a kids' TV show. Since Mary wants to be discreet about prying Murray from the game, she doesn't come out and say why she's there. When she offers Murray a ride home, Mr. Grant has had enough. "You're banished from this kingdom," he says, pushing her toward the pink castle door.

LIFE LESSON:

When in Doubt about the Right Thing to Do, Be Kind

In season 4, Lou finds himself in one of those positions where he knows the right thing to do, but it takes some effort for him to do it. It's the first Teddy Awards banquet since he and Edie broke up, and he invites her to go as his date. The good news is that she plans to be there. The bad news is she's going with someone else! Edie seems to be thriving in her new single life, while Lou still misses her. Maybe this event will be a good time to show Edie how well he's doing. "If she can get a date, I can get a date . . . Mary, get me a date!" Nowadays, HR wouldn't look kindly on a boss asking his colleague to get him a date, but back then it was a totally reasonable ask. Rhoda knows a nice, middle-aged widow from her dance class, Mrs. Dudley, who might be a good match for Lou. Indeed, when Mary calls her, Mrs. Dudley says she is happy to go to the banquet with Lou. But as the night of the banquet approaches, Lou is getting cold feet. He begs Mary to call Mrs. Dudley and cancel. "I am not going out with some woman I never met before," insists Lou. But Mary convinces him to change his mind.

The night of the banquet, Mrs. Dudley shows up . . . and it turns out she's a little old lady with gray hair and orthopedic shoes. It seems that Mary invited the wrong Mrs. Dudley. Lou is obviously shocked when he realizes that his date is this old lady, but he's cool enough that he doesn't freak out in front of her. He's momentarily at a loss for words. He doesn't want to hurt Mrs. Dudley's feelings, but he's clearly unnerved by the prospect of bringing her to the Teddy Awards dinner. This was his chance to show off a new date to Edie, who will be there with someone else.

He asks Mary to join him in the kitchen, which somehow manages to provide privacy even though it's separated from the rest of the apartment by just a stained glass window. Mary hands him a drink and apologizes. Lou responds sarcastically, "Please, there's no need to apologize. It's not your fault. All I said to you was, 'Get me a date!' I didn't specify what kind of date. How were you to know that I wanted somebody under ninety?"

Mary tries to explain. "You see, there are two Mrs. Dudleys."

"Mary, there are *thousands* of Mrs. Dudleys. Why *this* Mrs. Dudley? I can't take that little old lady to that dinner. My wife is going to be at that dinner. I can't walk in there with that . . . Mrs. Dudley."

Lou tries to explain the misunderstanding to Mrs. Dudley: "This dinner tonight is very important to me. You see, this will be the first time I have taken a woman out since my wife and I separated."

She's not getting his subtle hint. She tells him, "Believe me, Lou. Tonight is gonna do you a world of good." She thinks this is a real date—and why shouldn't she? She says, "Call me Martha," and tells him she got her dress just for the evening. How can he disappoint her?

"Why don't you just go through with it? She's a sweet, lovely lady. You have absolutely nothing to be embarrassed about," Mary says, and Lou is starting to see her point . . . until Ted shows up and ruins everything, as usual.

"Hey, who's the old lady?" he asks.

Leave it to kindhearted Georgette to accept the situation without seeing anything funny about it. When Mary introduces her to Martha, she innocently asks, "Have you and Mr. Grant been together long?" She looks at the world with childlike wonder (which sometimes makes her seem stupid), but in fact, she's quite insightful and nonjudgmental. (She's not ageist, like the rest of them.) Georgette is naturally good and seems to recognize the best qualities in everyone. She takes the time to get to know Martha and tells Lou, "Martha has had such an interesting life. Did you know she was a flower girl at Thomas Alva Edison's wedding?"

Lou does the right thing and brings Martha to the dinner, but he's clearly embarrassed about her and is in a rush to leave. He spends the whole evening trying to avoid Edie and her date. But, of course, Ted being his usual ignorant self brings Edie and her date over. It turns out he's a silver fox, a hunk of a man who towers over Lou and can pull off wearing a velvet tuxedo jacket. How can Lou compete with that? "Did you bring someone to the dinner?" Edie asks.

Lou pretends that Mary is his date and introduces Martha as a friend of Mary's. The moment that Edie walks away, Lou feels a pang of guilt. "What did I just do?"

"Well, it was a tough spot," says Mary.

"Not that tough."

It's not too late to set things right. Lou asks Martha to join him, and he escorts her over to Edie, where he proudly reintroduces her as his date. "Did you know that Martha was the flower girl at Thomas Alva Edison's wedding?" he brags, his arm now hanging around Martha's shoulder. He's no longer self-conscious about being seen with Martha. Lou asks Martha to dance, and they enjoy their evening together.

She's got some pep in her step for an eighty-year-old who says, "These old legs don't always do what I tell them to." Lou has chosen to act with kindness, and in doing so, he made it through his first date in twenty-five years (since before he and Edie were married) with grace.

LIFE LESSON:
Let People Know You Care about Them

Though he's happily married and is proud of his kids, Murray's life hasn't turned out the way he thought it would. Instead of being a successful playwright or author, he writes copy for the lowest-rated news program in Minneapolis, to be read aloud by an anchor who confuses *vegetarian* and *veterinarian*. He's a recovering gambling addict who barely makes enough money to support his family. Usually, he channels his anger into cynicism, which fuels the nonstop sarcastic banter and snarky comebacks directed at Ted and Sue Ann. For the most part, that helps him cope with his disappointment and malaise. But when he learns that a former classmate of his won a Pulitzer Prize, Murray falls into a depression.

"Hey, Mary, you ever feel like going out by yourself and getting bombed out of your mind?" asks Murray.

Mary recognizes her friend is in crisis. She takes him out for coffee to find out what's going on, but he can't put it into words. "He just sort of puts it into sighs," Mary explains to Mr. Grant. They grow increasingly concerned about Murray when he arrives three hours late to work. This is a guy who has never been three minutes late.

Next, there's a very bro-mantic moment. When Murray explains he skipped work to go to the movies, he tells Lou to fire him. "You don't need me. Nobody missed me." We expect Lou to bark at Murray, but this is when Lou shows his softer side. He tells Murray that it's fine if he's got to skip another day of work for another day at the movies.

Murray is having a midlife crisis. "I used to think that I might have a shot at a Pulitzer Prize or that I would become a concert pianist . . . But I'm forty years old. I'm here now, but where am I gonna be in ten years?"

Mary is so concerned about Murray that she asks Ted to be nice to him. "You've gotta show some sympathy until he snaps out of it."

Of course, we know now that people don't just snap out of depression, but considering Prozac was still two decades away, the gang is very understanding and supportive of Murray. Ted brings Murray back to his home, or what he calls "the silver fox's lair," in an effort to cheer him up and even tries to use puppets to get Murray to open up! Mary swings by to check on Murray and tries a different tactic, telling him, "I think that we've been all wrong about this whole thing. Why are we trying to cheer you up? If you feel sad, you should feel sad. I was a little sad myself today, and I know the last thing in the world I wanted was somebody trying to cheer me up. You should feel what you feel. If you're sad, be sad."

"Let's all be sad together," says Ted.

But Mary's really concerned. "Oh, Murray, don't be sad. When you're sad, it just makes me feel so sad." He fakes a smile just to please her because when the girl with the world-turning smile isn't smiling, nobody's smiling. She reminds him, "You got a good life. You got a wonderful family. You've got good friends who really care about you." This is the Mary effect: taking a nothing day and making it seem worthwhile.

"You did me a lot of good. I never realized so many people were affected by how I felt. It doesn't help much, but it sure makes me feel good," he says. Big hug!

Murray takes a lot of hits over the course of seven years. In the final season, when everybody in the newsroom except Murray wins a Teddy Award, Murray is a good sport. "I lost, but you won. I think we should celebrate." Back at Mary's apartment, Murray reads the speech he had prepared, telling them that the best part of awards is you can tell people what you really think about them. He tells Lou, "There's not a man alive that I have more respect for or whose respect means more to me." Then, he turns to Mary and tells her, "You do the impossible every day. You make people forget how beautiful you look because they're too busy realizing how beautiful you are." He even has a compliment for Ted: "I say a lot of things to you in the newsroom, but there's one thing I've never said: I'd miss you if you weren't there. You're filled with joy, love, and wonder. And I like you." Ted starts slobbering. Big hug!

LIFE LESSON:

Appreciate What You Have

When Ted has a mild heart attack on-air ("This is Ted Baxter saying, 'Good night, good news, and maybe goodbye.'"), it gives him a new perspective on life. The office gang visits him at the hospital, and they discover a completely different Ted. Gone is the pompous, self-involved, cheap, vain news anchor. In his place is an insightful man who appreciates his friends and the beauty of everyday moments. "I learned that life is short and you have to live for today," Ted says. "Too bad it took a heart attack to open my eyes. Oh, I've been such a fool. But from now on, I'm gonna spin a web of love, beauty, truth. I'm gonna savor each moment of life like some rare exotic delicacy, and I'm gonna treat every person like I'm never gonna see them again." He hugs each of them goodbye and kisses Murray's bald scalp.

Ted is noticing the wonder of the world, including little things—like salt. When he and Georgette come over to Mary's for dinner, Ted tells them, "I've been around salt all my life, but I never really paid attention to it."

Georgette is growing tired of this new Ted. "You showed me salt yesterday."

Meanwhile, the famously frugal Ted is suddenly generous with his money, which he tries to force on Mary. "What's money?" he asks. "Money's only measurement is the amount of joy it brings to the one you love."

The next day, Ted bounces into the office, asking, "Isn't it a glorious day?"

Just as we expect Mr. Grant to tell Ted to "knock it off," he surprises us by announcing, "Ted, you're making everybody crazy with this new attitude of yours. You're screwing up the whole newsroom—and Ted, I think it's terrific . . . I know this sounds stupid, but did any of us ever stop to think that Ted might be right?"

"Not for a second," jokes Murray.

But Mr. Grant is serious. "I mean it, Murray. When I was sitting in the park with the flowers and the trees and the children playing, I began to wonder if maybe there could be more important things in this world than putting on a news show. What's wrong with taking the time to enjoy life and people and things, nature? Why should we have to have a heart attack to appreciate things? What's wrong about being a little more appreciative?"

Mr. Grant tells Mary, "We've been working together now, Mary, for what, seven years? In all those years, did I ever tell you how wonderful you are, what a delight it is to be your friend?"

Mary tells Mr. Grant, "There are a lot of things like that that I never said to you either. I think you're a wonderful man. It's really great to be around you. You make life exciting and fun. I'm really glad I know you. You're a beautiful human being."

Mr. Grant and Mary embrace, and Murray gushes: "I've got a lovely wife, great kids, wonderful friends. I've got my health . . . I'm the luckiest man in the world."

Suddenly, Mr. Grant is noticing things he's never noticed before. He stops at the window to see the sunset. "I've been working here for twelve years trying to get out the news and not once did I look out the window and see that sunset," he says to Mary. Mr. Grant calls Murray and everyone else in the newsroom to look at the sunset. "Isn't it incredible?" Mr. Grant asks Ted.

"Yeah, I guess it's okay."

Mr. Grant realizes that Ted's new attitude has worn off. "I guess it always wears off," he says. "So it doesn't last forever; so it wears off. That's no reason not to appreciate it when it's here. We've got it. Let's make the most of it." The episode ends with Murray, Lou, and Mary holding each other and silently watching the sun go down. They realize this moment won't last, so they will savor it. A week later, they're all sniping at each other again. That's the magic of television!

QUIZ: How Well Do You Know *The Mary Tyler Moore Show*?

1. Which talk show host made a guest appearance on the show?

    a) Merv Griffin

    b) Phil Donahue

    c) Dick Cavett

    d) Johnny Carson

2. Where do Rhoda and Mary go on vacation?

    a) Puerto Rico

    b) Mexico

    c) Florida

    d) California

3. Who is Lou Grant's favorite movie star?

    a) Robert Redford

    b) Paul Newman

    c) John Wayne

    d) Clint Eastwood

4. Who cancels their appearance on *Talk of the Town*, a talk show Mary produces?

    a) Prince Charles

    b) Queen Elizabeth

    c) Prince Philip

    d) Dr. Ruth

5. In the sixth season, Ted Baxter auditions to be a quizmaster of which new TV game show?

    a) *The Fifty Thousand Dollar Pyramid*

    b) *The One Hundred Thousand Dollar Race*

    c) *Winner Takes All*

    d) *The Fifty Thousand Dollar Steeplechase*

6. Why does Mary have to go to the hospital?

    a) She's got to have her tonsils removed.

    b) She's got to have one tonsil removed.

    c) She's got a broken leg.

    d) She's just visiting someone.

7. What's the name of Mary's hometown?

    a) Roseburg, Minnesota

    b) Rosebud, Minnesota

    c) Rome, Minnesota

    d) It's never mentioned.

8. To make extra money, Murray starts moonlighting as a:

    a) taxi driver

    b) bartender

    c) referee

    d) stand-up comic

9. Phyllis often repeats her husband's sayings in which foreign language?

    a) Finnish

    b) Danish

    c) French

    d) Swedish

10. What's the name of the hip youth-oriented boutique where Mary and Rhoda shop?

    a) Shot Down in Ecuador, Junior

    b) Here Comes the Sun

    c) The Cat's Meow

    d) Easy Livin'

Answer Key:

1. d	5. d	9. d
2. b	6. b	10. a
3. c	7. a	
4. a	8. a	

0–3 correct answers: Shame on you. You need to watch more Mary Tyler Moore!

4–7 correct answers: Not bad. You know your Mary!

8–10 correct answers: Toss your hat up in the air! You're a Mary expert.

CHAPTER NINE

LOVE AND SEX

"I'm an experienced woman.
I've been around . . . Well, all right, I might
not've been around, but I've been . . . nearby."

—MARY RICHARDS

127

S he didn't shout it from the rooftops of Minneapolis or dish about it over Cosmopolitans like the single ladies on *Sex and the City* did two decades later, but there was no doubt about it: Mary Richards had sex. That in itself was groundbreaking considering that just a few years earlier, television rules mandated that she and her on-screen husband, Dick Van Dyke, had to sleep in separate beds on *The Dick Van Dyke Show*. But by 1970, with Mary Richards thirty years old and coming off of a long-term relationship, nobody would buy that she was a virgin. The writers understood that, and though it was never explicitly stated, it was definitely implied.

In their original twenty-one-page proposal for the show, Brooks and Burns described their vision of the Mary Richards character, saying that she "seems especially wholesome when contrasted with those around her. (We'll let you in on a secret that's for our eyes only. Mary is not a virgin. This becomes a very wholesome quality when you realize that Rhoda is not a virgin many times over.)" In fact, Mary's wholesome, WASPish small-town girl-next-door quality is exactly what allowed the writers to put some risqué dialogue in her mouth. Mary Richards was a good girl, so somehow she got a pass. As *People* magazine noted in 1974, "Mary Tyler Moore does indeed have sex appeal, but it is the kind that does not make her own sex nervous, because it is wholesome. Men grow googly-eyed watching Mary of the blazing Irish smile and the tight-tight slacks, and wives don't mind because she is so plainly a Good Scout."

Valerie Harper once explained, "Mary's wholesome, but she's not too wholesome. I mean, for example, she likes a great big glass of cold milk . . . to wash down her birth control pill." Just when we think Mary is innocent, she surprises us with a suggestive comment or a hint that she's much more experienced than we might assume. For example, in one early episode, Mary produces a documentary for the station called "What's Your Sexual IQ?" When Rhoda lets on that she only got forty-seven out of one hundred, Mary teases, "Who cares if you didn't pass it? I know that I certainly don't mind that I got a ninety." Mary brags she would have gotten one hundred except she wears flannel pajamas.

"How do you like that? I flunked the sexual IQ test, and I pass the national driver's test—and Mary, I'm a lousy driver," says Rhoda.

As the '70s rolled on, sexual attitudes around the country continued to evolve. But the sexual revolution hadn't yet hit prime-time network television. Mary wasn't invited to any key parties (as far as we know). Treva Silverman, one of the early writers for the show, later joked, "Mary Goes to the Playboy Mansion, I think, was an idea whose time had never come. 'Mary swims topless, as Hugh Hefner looks fondly on' was not going to happen."

The times were changing, but not that fast—at least on TV. Remember, it was only in 1972 that an episode of *All in the Family* included the sound of a toilet flushing. In 1975, Cher became the first woman in prime time to show her navel—and it was a huge controversy! Before that, CBS had made *I Dream of Jeannie* star Barbara Eden pull her genie pants up to cover her navel during that show's 1965–1970 run.

When a real-life Chicago journalist suggested that Mary Richards was "undersexed," writer Susan Silver worked the question into an episode in season 3. Mary asks Rhoda, "Do you think I'm undersexed?"

"I hope so," Rhoda answers. "I'd like to think there's one thing I'm better at than you are." Mary's asking because her date wanted to spend the night, but she said no. Mary wondering aloud about sex—and whether she got enough of it—was pretty daring for television of the era. A few episodes later, Mary gets gussied up for a dinner party. The next time we see her, she's arriving home in the morning wearing the same outfit! When Rhoda knocks on Mary's door hoping to get a ride to work, she notices that Mary is still dressed in her sequined evening wear. When Mary explains that she just got home, Rhoda smiles and says, "You must have had some great time."

"Look, Rhoda, whatever I did, it's my business."

Rhoda replies, "That good, huh?"

It seems Mary is feeling a little defensive because her parents have just moved to Minneapolis—and it's too close for comfort. When they grill her about what she was doing until 8:27 a.m., she sets a firm boundary and tells them, "I am over thirty years old. I don't have to answer that." They're not happy about it, but her parents have no choice in the matter. Their daughter is a grown woman who doesn't need her parents' permission to stay out all night. She can decide on her own when and where and if she wants to have sex. And she doesn't have to explain her choices to anyone. As she tells Rhoda, "I'd just like to be able to go out and stay out all night if I feel like it."

It was such a big deal for Mary to stay out all night that it actually got written into the script of another groundbreaking feminist show. On Norman Lear's *Maude*, the title character (Bea Arthur) took note: "All night? *Our little Mary?*" No doubt, all over the country, people were asking the same question. Just a few episodes later, when Mary's mother is leaving Mary's apartment, she turns back and calls out, "Don't forget to take your pill!"

Both Mary and her father answer simultaneously, "I won't!" Her father turns to look at Mary, who has a guilty look on her face—and we know for sure she means the Pill. The studio audience gets it too. You can hear them cracking up. Up until then, nobody had referred to birth control on a sitcom—and especially not a nice girl like Mary. Perhaps it was her nice girl status that allowed Mary to get away with it. "Had it had something to do with Rhoda, it wouldn't have had that effect, because Rhoda was something of a rebel. If Mary was taking the Pill, it gave the stamp of approval for sexuality," said writer Treva Silverman. This was pretty bold stuff considering the birth control pill had won federal approval in 1960, but it wasn't until 1972 that a Supreme Court decision made it available to unmarried women like Mary.

Still, even though Mary's a grown woman, the guys in the office still feel protective of her. When Mary says she wants to volunteer as a Big Sister for juvenile delinquents, Murray warns her: "Mary, these girls have been around. You don't know what kind of trouble they've been in. Some of these girls may have, uh, dated heavily."

MARY: What are you trying to say? That I haven't lived enough? That I'm too naive to be a Big Sister?

MURRAY: Let's face it, Mary. You're not what I would call an experienced woman.

MARY: Murray! You have no idea how experienced or inexperienced I am. I mean sure, true, I'm not what you would call a wild woman, but I'm hardly innocent. I've been around. All right, I might not have been around, but I've been nearby.

By the fifth season, when Mary and Sue Ann return from the broadcasters' convention in Chicago, the guys in the office are curious to hear what happened—especially because when Lou had phoned their hotel room, it sounded like they were having a party. "I wanted to explain to you about that phone call," Mary says to Mr. Grant.

"Why? Because when I called you, all I could hear was shrieks and giggles and the sound of drunken laughter," he says.

Mary explains that there's a perfectly logical explanation for what he heard: "We were having an orgy." She smiles and walks away, leaving the men to guess whether she's joking or not.

Ted laughs nervously. "You were kidding, weren't you, Mary?" But she smiles and ignores him. Ted, Murray, and Lou aren't sure what to think. Our little Mary? An orgy? "She's got to be kidding," Ted says, trying to convince himself. But Mary keeps them guessing.

LIFE LESSON:

Take Chances in Love and Romance

Sure, you might get hurt, but it's worth the risk. That's the advice Mary gives to Ted. Following a guest appearance on Chuckles the Clown's show, Ted is acting weirder than usual. He's wearing a fake mustache until his real one grows in, and he seems to be sneaking around the office and swiping the single rose that Mary always has on her desk. Rhoda figures it out: he's in love with Betty Bowerchuck (Arlene Golonka), Chuckles's assistant and daughter. Mary has a heart-to-heart with Ted, where she pushes him to be emotionally honest. It's a rare moment when Ted Baxter reveals his deep fears without any silly jokes or stupid comments. Mary is direct with Ted and asks him why he's lied and told Betty that the company manual said they can't date. Ted says there should be a rule about dating coworkers since "it gets in the way of the work." But Mary knows Ted well enough to know that there's more to it. He's clearly really into Betty, so what's the problem?

Ted keeps coming up with reasons, but Mary keeps pressing him to go deeper and be emotionally honest. Finally, he reveals the insecurity lurking beneath his nonstop bravado. He admits to Mary:

> **TED:** What if she really doesn't love me? What if I get engaged to her and tell everyone and even have my engagement picture in the paper, and then she dumps me for somebody? How would I look? Pretty silly, right?
>
> **MARY:** Well, Ted, that's one of the chances you have to take.

TED: That's easy for you to say. You've never been dumped by somebody.

MARY: Sooner or later, everyone gets rejected.

TED: Not me. You don't love somebody; you don't get rejected.

MARY: You don't get loved either.

When Ted says he's afraid of being hurt, Mary tells him, "Being hurt is part of life. It's part of love." Mary says that even she's been hurt a couple of times but that it was a "good hurt. It wasn't permanent or anything. Here I am."

Mary reminds us that it's worth taking a chance on love. She proves her point in a later episode when she takes yet another chance on Tom Vernon (Joseph Campanella), an old boyfriend who's broken her heart several times over. She hasn't seen him in two and a half years and has finally gotten over him. When Tom shows up in Minneapolis wanting to rekindle the old flame with Mary, at first, she avoids seeing him since she doesn't want to get hurt. But after a pep talk from Rhoda, who tells her to go for it, Mary takes another chance and agrees to a date. When he arrives at her apartment, she's trying to keep boundaries between them and is eager to go out to dinner. But he wants to stay and "get reacquainted." She tries to hold back for fear of being hurt again, but Tom is really charming, and she can't resist. Once he kisses her—a real long, deep kiss—she changes her mind about going out. Let's order in! Mary's getting lucky tonight. Though it's not explicitly stated (or shown), clearly Mary and Tom spent the night together. And then—just like Tom—he doesn't call her the next day at work like he promised he would.

That night, he shows up to her apartment unannounced with pizza for dinner. Clearly, he plans another night of "getting reacquainted" with Mary. But she's annoyed that he didn't call like he said he would. And he forgot she hates anchovies! They have a frank discussion about their relationship, which clearly isn't working for Mary.

Mary took a chance on Tom, and though it didn't work out in the end, at least she knows where things stand—and they "got reacquainted." Even if it's not a long-term arrangement, Mary and Tom have chemistry, maybe more than she has with any of her dates.

Mary continues to take chances on love. In the second-to-last episode of the series, Mary and her date return to her apartment after a nice evening. She offers him coffee, and he takes that as an invitation to undress. She's furious that he'd just assume she was interested. She quickly does the math and realizes that she's been on two thousand dates and most of them were awful.

"They haven't all been bad. There have been some good ones, about ten percent—that's two hundred really fine ones. And eighteen hundred rotten ones! I am thinking of all the rituals of dating and for what? All the hours spent getting through the evening, saying all those things I have to say. I mean, I've just had it with all these games over and over again. I'm too old for this."

She apologizes for her rant, and her date says her frankness is refreshing. She says maybe they can start over. He gets the wrong idea and starts taking his shirt off again! At that point, she opens the door and yells, "Out!"

The next day, Mary vents to Georgette. "Me, men, dating . . . You know how you go along thinking someday you'll meet the right person. For the first time, I'm not sure that's gonna happen. I'm not even sure he exists—at least not the kind of man I'm talking about." Georgette suggests she date Mr. Grant. "Me date Lou Grant? That's ridiculous," Mary says, but then she gets to thinking, *Why not?* He does meet her criteria of "someone who doesn't care about how I look because he's more concerned with who I am, somebody strong and intelligent who respects me, who I can respect, who has gentleness in him." As long as she's taking a chance on love, why not take a chance with Mr. Grant— even if it's awkward?

When Mary asks Mr. Grant out on a date, he looks at her as if she's asked him a question in German. He says, "You want to go out on a date with *me*? You're out of your mind . . . We're not a man and a woman. We're friends. We respect each other. We care for each other. We care a great deal. How can two people who feel like that date each other?" They realize how ridiculous that sounds and decide to try a real date. What's the worst that can happen?

For some, this is the episode that they were waiting for, and for others, this is the episode that never should have happened. Nowadays, HR would never let this happen.

The moment Mr. Grant (she tries to call him Lou, but it's so awkward) arrives at her apartment with several bouquets of flowers (since he doesn't know her favorite), they suddenly find themselves unable to have a normal conversation. While they usually get along famously, in this new situation, they're at a loss. It's just super awkward! Eventually, they figure they might as well test out the chemistry just to be sure. They share a tentative kiss and then immediately break into laughter.

MR. GRANT: I think we both figured something out in record time. This will never work.

MARY: Never in a million years.

Well, at least they got that out of their system! Mary took a chance. It didn't pay off, but now she knows.

MTM Trivia: *Ed Asner and Mary Tyler Moore had never worked together before even though they were both in the cast of Elvis's last feature film,* Change of Habit. *(Moore played a nun!) They weren't in any scenes together and never had the chance to meet before* The Mary Tyler Moore Show.

LIFE LESSON:
Take the Shame Out of Sex

Even though Mary is often uptight about sex, she is surprisingly sex positive. She lectures Mr. Grant about slut-shaming his new girl-friend, Charlene (Sheree North), a gorgeous lounge singer—although she doesn't use the term *slut-shaming*! Mr. Grant is so crazy about Charlene he bounces into the office humming a happy tune. He's also jazzed up his wardrobe with a velvet blazer and a turtleneck instead of his usual poorly fitted suit. Lou's in love! Mary meets Charlene and thinks she's terrific. "She's one of the warmest, nicest, most interesting people I've ever met," she tells Murray and Ted. She probably should have stopped there. Instead, she continues. "She was on the road with a band when she was sixteen years old. And one of her husbands pitched in both major leagues. She was the only girl on a marine base in Korea."

The guys tease Lou about how experienced his new girlfriend is. "You old son of a gun. I never pictured you with a band stewardess," says Murray.

"On the road when she was sixteen. Isn't that against the law?" asks Ted. Lou understands what his colleagues are getting at. Charlene has been around.

Lou stops calling Charlene and falls into a deep funk. When Mary asks why he has ghosted Charlene, he explains: "I just can't see myself with that sort of woman."

"What sort of woman?" Mary asks.

"I can't discuss the sort of woman she is with the sort of woman you are. That's the sort of woman she is."

But Mary isn't having any of it. "Are you telling me that you're breaking up with Charlene because she's known some other men?"

"Not some other men, *lots* of other men."

Mary asks, "What's the cutoff point, Mr. Grant? Is there some number? I'd really like to know. How many men is a woman allowed to have before she becomes 'that kind of woman'?" It's a rhetorical question, but Mr. Grant's got an answer for Mary: six!

But eventually, Mary's message sinks in, and Lou visits Charlene at the piano bar to try to work things out. Clearly, Lou has been doing some serious introspection. He digs deep and comes up with this gem: "Listen—I got to tell you the truth. Whatever I was saying before about your past, forget it. Forget it. It's not your past that's bothering me. It's my past. I haven't even got one. I guess I was trying to tell myself that you weren't good enough for me. The truth is I was afraid that I wasn't going to be good enough for you." She assures him that that won't be the case. By then, Charlene is playing the piano, and she, Lou, and the customers circle around the piano to sing along to "You Made Me Love You." It's genuinely sweet.

Speaking of "that sort of woman," when newsroom nymphomaniac Sue Ann Nivens swoops in and steals Phyllis's husband in the first episode of season 4, it spices the show up with double entendres and sexual innuendo. Sue Ann is definitely "that sort of woman," and she's not shy about advertising it. The show's cocreator Allan Burns later described the character as "cloyingly sweet on the surface and something of a dragon underneath, with a tinge of nymphomania," and, no doubt, he meant that as a compliment. Betty White told the *Los Angeles Times* back in 1973 that she loved playing such a sexually liberated woman. "She's not only a bitch but a nympho. She can't keep her hands off any man, not even Ted [Baxter]. I've been waiting all my life for a part like this."

There's no question that middle-aged, unmarried Sue Ann is not a virgin. She's got a dirty mind and is not afraid to let her coworkers know it. In one episode, when Sue Ann comments on the wallpaper in the men's room at WJM, Mary asks, "Did you crash the men's room?"

Her reply? "Of course not . . . I went as somebody's guest." Some of her comments are quite racy (and today might be considered problematic). When Murray says, "Being fired is like being violated," Sue Ann quips, "Leave it to Murray to find a bright spot in all of this." When Lou isn't sure what to get Sue Ann for her birthday, Murray quips, "What do you get for the woman who's had everyone?"

Even on-air, Sue Ann's cheery domestic goddess persona is focused on sex: "This is your Happy Homemaker reminding you that a woman who does a good job in the kitchen is sure to reap her rewards in other parts of the house." Wink, wink. Another time, she tells Mary about a show she's doing on single girls. "The topic is 'What Turns a Man On.' Now, of course, I have lots of ideas, but I thought you might have a few that I could actually say on television."

Sue Ann is vocal about her sexual desire—especially for Lou. When Mary suggests that Lou needs to lose weight, Sue Ann tells him, "Your body is perfect. I wouldn't touch it. If I did, I wouldn't stop." Sue Ann is excited to learn that both she and Lou will be attending the broadcasters' convention in Chicago. She says suggestively to Lou, "We'll see *everything*. We'll do *everything*. It will give us something to remember and talk about for years afterward." Lou isn't interested. Sue Ann's sexuality makes Lou very nervous. Suddenly, he finds he's too busy to attend the convention and sends Mary instead.

It takes Sue Ann a couple of seasons before she manages to bed Lou near the end of season 6, in one of the series's best episodes, "Once I Had a Secret Love." Lou stumbles into the office still drunk one morning and snaps at Mary to get rid of the liquor around the office. "I do crazy things when I'm drunk . . . Do you know what it's like to wake up next to a stranger?" he asks Mary.

"Sure," she says. Nervous laughter—has Mary had a one-night stand with a stranger? Mary adds, "Well, I can certainly imagine." Mr. Grant says he feels so bad because of who the woman is. "It doesn't matter who the woman is," says Mary. "Who's the woman?"

At that point, Mary notices Mr. Grant isn't wearing any socks. Right then, Sue Ann strolls in with a satisfied grin on her face. "I didn't sleep a wink all night. I feel wonderful!" She hands Lou his socks—which she cleaned, of course. Mary can't stop laughing.

"This concludes the entertainment part of this program," says Mr. Grant, who asks Sue Ann not to tell anyone "what happened last night."

"Oh, Lou, you silly, everyone will know by the roses in your cheeks!"

Sue Ann's sexual appetite was often played for laughs. A single, middle-aged woman aggressively pursuing sex—rather than marriage—was daring for the time. Remember her frilly pink boudoir, with its mirrors on the ceiling, vibrating bed, and a remote

Mary Richards's Boyfriends

Mary had so many boyfriends. What was wrong with them? We review some of the memorable guys she dated throughout the series—and rank them from best to worst.

Dan Whitfield (Michael Tolan): This handsome journalism teacher is one of the best guys Mary dates. Mary's family and friends are crazy about him, and he is crazy about Mary. Although she loves Dan—maybe more than any man she has ever known—Mary needs more time to figure out if they're meant to be together in the long run. Ironically, if he wasn't in such a rush to get married, Dan and Mary might actually have had a future together.

Tom Vernon (Joseph Campanella): Tom Vernon is Mary's former sweetheart, the one who got away. He's hurt her so many times in the past, and she's afraid to give him the chance to hurt her again. But there's real chemistry between them, and she can't resist. He doesn't want a commitment, but at least they can enjoy the time they have together.

Eric Matthews (Hamilton Camp): When Mary meets bestselling author Eric Matthews, he's seated and ready to be interviewed. The editors will splice in Ted as the interviewer later. Eric seems to be just Mary's type: he's intelligent and funny. After the interview ends, he asks Mary out for a date, and she doesn't hesitate to accept. Once they stand up to leave, she realizes she's towering above him. He barely rises above her shoulders—and that's if she's wearing flats! She realizes that she's a "height bigot," and she tries to change her mind about him, but she can't get over the height difference.

They've got chemistry, and he seems like maybe the best guy she's met, but clearly, she's never gonna get over his height.

Doug Slaughter (Lew Ayres): Mary agrees to go out on a date with a distinguished, well-traveled older gentleman, who turns out to be Murray's father, Doug. He's thirty-one years older than she is, but she doesn't mind. Despite his advanced age, Doug's a catch. He's handsome, worldly, and charming (much more so than Murray!). The only problem is that he's not interested. After Mary makes an impassioned speech at a party about how age doesn't matter, he dumps her for someone else. He's maybe the only guy who Mary dates who rejects her.

Joe Warner (Ted Bessell): Best known for his role of Donald, Ann Marie's (Marlo Thomas) fiancé on *That Girl*, Ted Bessell plays Joe Warner, one of Mary's most serious boyfriends. A construction executive who is into Mary and public displays of affection, he sometimes makes modest Mary feel uncomfortable. He's also not a fan of monogamy, as she discovers when she shows up at his apartment to profess her love for him, only to find he's got another woman over. He's charming, but don't trust him. He's a player!

Ken Arnold (Laurence Luckinbill): Ken Arnold is a single dad who is crazy about his son, Stevie, even though Mary isn't. He's cute, but it's not going to work, since Stevie is a nightmare. In real life, Luckinbill married Lucie Arnaz, the daughter of Desi Arnaz and Lucille Ball, in 1980. He's had a full career, including perhaps his most famous role as Spock's half-brother, Sybok, in *Star Trek V*.

Paul Van Dillen (Robert Wolders): Mary dates a gorgeous ski instructor, but everyone gives her a hard time about going out with him because he's so good looking. Mr. Grant tells Mary, "I hate to tell you this, but he's prettier than you are." He's handsome and charming, and Mary is enjoying the arm candy. But her coworkers won't let up, so it won't work in the long run. Trivia tidbit: Wolders was Audrey Hepburn's longtime companion.

Stephen Linder (Peter Strauss): Mary meets a fun, young guy— *young* being the key word, or as Rhoda puts it, "He's a little short . . . in the age department." Mr. Grant tells Mary she's ruining her life over this young guy, and Mary pushes back, telling him, "I find this extremely none of your business." Mary says she doesn't mind that Stephen is a few years younger than her, but she changes her mind when she finds out Stephen is eight years younger. Maybe in a few years the age difference won't matter as much? Anyway, he's sweet.

Howard Arnell (Richard Schaal): Howard is super intense and overbearing. Mary breaks up with him once, but he later shows up at her high school reunion. Another stalker type!

Paul Arnell (Richard Schaal): Paul is Howard Arnell's much more low-key and charming brother. Unfortunately, the brothers' parents don't approve of the match, since they feel Mary is "Howard's girl." Too bad, because he's a good guy.

Wes Callison (Jerry Van Dyke, Dick's brother): Wes is a writer for *The Chuckles the Clown Show*, but what he really wants to do is be a stand-up comic. Unfortunately, he's not funny. Also, he's sort of a sad sack. He's way more into Mary than she is him. She's basically nice to him because she doesn't want to hurt his feelings. Mary seems to date him out of pity, which is never a good idea! When he proposes to her, Mary has no choice but to set him straight. This is never gonna happen, dude! You're way out of your league.

Bill (Angus Duncan): Bill is Mary's long-term ex-boyfriend, the one who prompted her move to Minneapolis in the first place. He dated Mary throughout med school and residency only to break up with her as soon as he became a full-fledged doctor. He only appears in the first episode, in which Mary tells him she's doing fine without him. At least he does the right thing and doesn't show up again. What a jerk!

Mark Whitfield (Peter Haskell): Mark is a local newspaper columnist who interviews Mary for his column. During their interview, he asks her out—if she says no, the interview might not be favorable. He puts her to work taking shorthand and asks if she can type up her own interview! Hard pass.

Warren Sturges (Stuart Margolin): Rhoda's boyfriend sets Mary up with a guy named Warren, who won't take no for an answer. He even handcuffs her to him so she'll agree to go out with him. Again, Mary is afraid to hurt his feelings. This guy is a total nightmare. Today he'd be considered a stalker. She eventually tells him to back off, but by then, he's already found another woman to pester. Loser!

control to cue up the sweeping romantic music? And remember Murray's response when he saw it? "Did you decorate it yourself? Or did you have a sex maniac come in?" Looking back, Sue Ann was merely ahead of her time in that she wasn't ashamed of her sex drive. Or, as Sue Ann might say, "I love sex. Don't hold it against me—then again, go ahead and hold it against me."

LIFE LESSON:
Don't Settle for Less Than You Deserve

═══════

It's hard to believe Mary is still single since every man she meets seems to fall instantly in love with her. When Bess's twelve-year-old boyfriend meets Mary, he becomes infatuated with her and is convinced they're meant to be together. The professor of the night class in journalism she and Rhoda are taking falls for her, as does her tax auditor, a new cameraman for the show, the journalist who interviews her for a newspaper profile, her mechanic, Ted, several of Rhoda's boyfriends, her lawyer, her new neighbor, and even happily married Murray! No straight man seems to be able to resist her charms. A charming architect falls for her—and so does his grown son. But nobody is good enough for our Mary.

In one of the final episodes of the series, at the end of a long day in the office, Lou, Murray, and Ted have a drink in Lou's office. The talk somehow turns to Mary's marital status. "How do you figure a terrific woman like Mary never got married?" Ted asks.

"I don't know. She probably just never met the right guy yet, that's all. She deserves the best," says Lou.

Murray adds, "The only problem is maybe there isn't anyone good enough for her. I think Mary should hold out 'til she meets the perfect guy." Clearly, that's how Mary feels as well since she certainly has her pick of eligible bachelors during the course of the series.

There are a couple of guys she's semiserious about who show up more than once, but most of her dates disappear after one episode. Mary wants most of the dates to disappear! Then there are the guys who don't get the message when Mary tries to let them down gently. Many of the guys she dates are obvious jerks or losers, and a number of them pursue Mary even though she's clearly not interested. Then there are some downright creeps—or guys who use their professional position to pressure Mary to date them, like the IRS guy who crushes hard on her, saying, "I've enjoyed doing you more than anybody I've done before." No doubt that sort of behavior would be considered sexual harassment today, but back then, it was played for laughs—and was pretty funny.

Until *The Mary Tyler Moore Show*, unmarried women in prime time were old maids, objects of pity. But that's the great thing about Mary—she's looking for love, but she's not willing to settle for less than she deserves. She's not desperate to get married and isn't putting her life on hold for anyone. Also, it's not as if she's sitting home alone waiting for the phone to ring. In fact, when she's pursued by an assistant to the governor, he keeps rescheduling their dates. He seems like a catch, but it's not worth the hassle. Every time they make plans, he cancels. Her time is more valuable than that. She's not that desperate for a date. After all, he's the one who pursued her. "What do I want to get involved with someone like that for?" she asks Rhoda. She tells him she's not interested.

Mary has a full life even without all the guys who are falling all over themselves trying to land a date with her. Several boyfriends propose to her over the course of the series. But there's always a reason she knows it won't work, and we love her for prioritizing her needs. She's not in a rush to marry just for the sake of it or because it's expected. For example, there was the time that Dan Whitfield (Michael Tolan), the tall, dark, and handsome journalism professor Mary once dated, breaks his engagement to another woman—during the engagement party. Mary and Dan start dating again, and he wines and dines her. But something seems off. Lying on her couch as if she's in a therapy session and Rhoda's her therapist, Mary gripes, "Everybody gets along just great. Dan and Dad are the best of pals. Dan's folks love me. I love his folks. His folks love my folks. My folks love his folks. I think Dan's the greatest guy I've ever known. There's just one problem: I think he's going to ask me to marry him."

"That's the very least you can do after you busted his engagement!" says Rhoda. "Don't you love him?"

Mary isn't sure. She needs time. Why rush into things? Rhoda points out that Dan clearly loves her, but Mary isn't so sure. After all, he was just professing his love to his ex-fiancée too. "He couldn't have loved her that much," says Mary. She's so right! "I think he's just in a mood to be married, but I'm not. Not right now anyway, I don't think."

Rhoda understands. "You do, but you don't, but you might."

At the newsroom, the gang gushes about how great Dan is. Lou calls him a "heck of a guy." Murray says, "You don't find guys like that every day." Mary's getting testy. Everyone keeps telling her how great Dan is. It's so annoying! Mr. Grant can tell that something is bothering Mary. Why isn't she crazy about Dan?

She explains, "Everybody thinks Dan is a great guy, and I think that he's going to ask me to marry him, but I don't know if I want to." She starts crying to Mr. Grant. "It just seems like something is missing."

Mr. Grant: "You're over thirty. If you're looking for that head-over-heels thing, that could be a long wait . . . Head-over-heels may never happen."

But Mary's fine taking that risk. She knows there's no point in partnering up unless she's really in love. She's having fun with Dan, but she's in no rush to commit. When Dan asks her to marry him, she replies, "I know that what I'm about to say may sound a little, you know, negative, but, uh, no."

He laughs. He thinks she's joking. "We know that you said that because you're scared to make a commitment," he tells her.

"No," she answers. "I admit that back when I thought that someday I had to get married it would have scared me, but now that I know that

I don't have to get married, it doesn't scare me." Mary says she cares for him and would like to have some time before jumping into marriage.

"I'm ready now," he says.

"But, Dan, I'm not . . . I've been thinking about this all week long, and I figured if I have to think about it, then I'm not ready." Mary is so right! Back at her apartment, Mary tells Rhoda about how she turned down Dan's proposal. "I think he was surprised to find out that I am not living my life in a constant search for the right man to marry. You know something? I was pretty surprised to find that out myself." In turning down Dan, Mary is putting herself first. She doesn't need to rush into marriage—even though she's over thirty. She realizes she can have a full love—and sex—life without getting married. Now that's a truly liberated woman!

CHAPTER TEN:

PUTTING IT ALL TOGETHER

"I treasure you people."

—LOU GRANT

The CBS mustaches had hated it. The first run-through had been a disaster. The initial reviews were terrible. However, *The Mary Tyler Moore Show* managed to stay on the air and eventually become one of the most successful—and most iconic—shows on television. Throughout its seven-year run from 1970 to 1977, it consistently ranked in the top twenty TV shows, often among the top ten. Along the way, it won three Golden Globes and racked up twenty-nine Emmy Awards—including three for outstanding comedy series. In fact, it held the record for most Emmys for a comedy series until *Frasier* earned its thirtieth Emmy in 2002. When the show went off the air in 1977, it was honored with a Peabody Award, one of the highest recognitions in media. The Peabody committee said the show "had established the benchmark by which all situation comedies must be judged" and praised it "for a consistent standard of excellence—and for a sympathetic portrayal of a career woman in today's changing society."

Along with *All in the Family*, *M*A*S*H**, *The Bob Newhart Show*, and *The Carol Burnett Show*, *The Mary Tyler Moore Show* was an essential element of one of the most successful TV blocks of all time. TV critics refer to the CBS Saturday-night lineup in the mid-1970s as the Holy Grail or the gold standard for TV programming. *The Los Angeles Times* has referred to that lineup as "a high-water mark for quality television," with former *LA Times* TV critic Howard Rosenberg writing in 2000 that the CBS Saturday-night programming block featuring

Mary "may have been the single most hilarious evening of TV comedy ever." These shows weren't just critically successful; they were commercial blockbusters. At its height, nearly half the TV-watching public in America stayed home on Saturday night to watch the CBS lineup. Remember, before VHS, DVDs, on-demand, streaming services, and TIVO, there was "appointment" television—which meant if you missed an episode, you'd have to wait until it showed up in reruns. As *Time* magazine noted when the finale aired, "*The Mary Tyler Moore Show* changed the nature of Saturday nights; it even became fashionable to spend them at home." The mid-1970s CBS Saturday-night lineup came to define the notion of watercooler TV, where everyone knew it would be a topic of discussion around the office watercooler on Monday morning, so they couldn't miss it on Saturday night. Talk about must-see TV!

By 1974, viewership for *The Mary Tyler Moore Show* ballooned to forty-three million. That's more than three times as many people as tuned in to watch the premiere of the final season of HBO's megahit *Game of Thrones*, and that was a series best. Mary was getting that number every week! Of course, back then, there were only three broadcast networks and, therefore, a lot less competition. And with new characters like Georgette and Aunt Flo mixing up the chemistry, people kept on tuning in, week after week. Yet three years later, thirty million viewers tuned in to watch Mary and her castmates say goodbye.

MTM Enterprises and Beyond

The Mary Tyler Moore Show was the first show from MTM Enterprises, the production company that Moore and her then husband, TV executive Grant Tinker, formed in 1969, and it set the bar high. In an impressive feat, throughout the 1970s, MTM generated several successful shows featuring characters spun off from *The Mary Tyler Moore Show*, including the sitcoms *Rhoda* and *Phyllis* and the one-hour drama *Lou Grant*. *Lou Grant* was unusual for being the rare one-hour drama spun off from a half-hour sitcom.

MTM was an industry force, with eight comedies in production. Because Tinker was known to hire writers he trusted and give them freedom to create, MTM was dubbed "Camelot for writers." With the critically acclaimed *Hill Street Blues*, the groundbreaking police drama, MTM expanded its focus from comedy to drama with great success. Its debut season won the show eight Emmy Awards, a debut season record at the time. (Later surpassed by *The West Wing*.)

Other pedigreed programs from MTM include *The Bob Newhart Show*, *Newhart*, *The White Shadow*, *Evening Shade*, *WKRP in Cincinnati*, *Remington Steele*, and *St. Elsewhere*. The MTM logo—a take-off on MGM's featuring a meowing tabby cat (named Mimsie) in place of the roaring lion—came to represent quality television. Over the years, there were variants on the logo with Mimsie often representing the topic or theme of each show. For instance, when Mimsie appeared at the end of

The Bob Newhart Show, she said, "Meow," in Newhart's deadpan voice. For WKRP, which is set at a radio station in Cincinnati, Mimsie appeared to be spinning on a record player. At the end of the series finale of the medical drama *St. Elsewhere* in 1988, Mimsie is shown hooked up to an IV with a heart monitor. As the credits roll, the heart monitor beeps and then flatlines, marking the end of the show and Mimsie's impending death. Mimsie died, at age twenty, shortly after the episode aired.

In 1978, four former MTM Enterprises employees—James L. Brooks, David Davis, Stan Daniels, and Ed Weinberger—created their own production company, which produced the TV show *Taxi*. Like *The Mary Tyler Moore Show*, it was a character-driven workplace ensemble that took on social issues of the day in a humorous, organic way. Next to Louie De Palma, the nasty boss played by Danny DeVito on *Taxi*, Lou Grant is a puppy dog. In 1982, when ABC cancelled the critically acclaimed low-rated show, Tinker saved it by putting it on NBC, where it ran for one more season.

In 1981, when Tinker and Moore divorced, he took the helm at NBC as chairman and CEO. In order to avoid any conflicts of interest, he sold his stake in MTM to Moore. During his tenure at NBC, he brought the network from last place to first place with hit shows such as *Family Ties*, *The Cosby Show*, *Cheers*, *L.A. Law*, *The Golden Girls* (featuring Betty White), and *Night Court*. Moore sold her shares in the company for $113 million in 1988. The MTM library assets were transferred to 20th Century Fox Television.

Brooks moved into feature film work in 1979 with *Starting Over*, which he cowrote and coproduced. His directorial debut was the tear-jerking relationship drama *Terms of Endearment*, which he also wrote and produced, earning him three Academy Awards (for Best Picture, Best Director, and Best Adapted Screenplay). Starring Shirley MacLaine, Debra Winger, and Jack Nicholson, the film won an Academy Award for all three leads. Brooks's next film, *Broadcast News*, was based on his journalistic experiences. In 1984, Brooks founded the television and film company Gracie Films. He went on to direct the Oscar-nominated romantic comedy *As Good as It Gets*, which earned Academy Awards for its two leads, Helen Hunt and Jack Nicholson. Brooks's Gracie Films produced *The Tracey Ullman Show*. When Brooks hired cartoonist Matt Groening for a series of animated shorts for the show, it led to *The Simpsons*, which has been on the air since 1989, surpassing *Gunsmoke* as the longest-running scripted TV series. Over the years, Brooks has served as a mentor for writer-directors including Cameron Crowe (*Say Anything*) and Wes Anderson and Owen Wilson (*Bottle Rocket*).

In 1992, Nickelodeon's adult-focused network, Nick at Nite, purchased the rights to most of the MTM library through 2003. They brought *The Mary Tyler Moore Show* back to prime time, where it resonated with baby boomer parents and also introduced a new generation of Gen X-ers and millennials to the charms of Mary and her TV family. Besides *Mary Tyler Moore*, Nick at Nite also bought exclusive rights to the spin-offs *Rhoda* and *Phyllis*, as well as the critically acclaimed MTM dramas *Hill Street Blues* and *St. Elsewhere*. Nick at Nite called its debut of *The Mary Tyler Moore Show* the "Marython," the network's name for a marathon of Mary. Some have credited Nick at Nite with creating the idea of programming marathons, a precursor to binge-watching. In the mid-1990s, Nick at Nite's "Very, Very Nick at Nite" programming block focused on a different theme each week. One week, entitled "Very, Very Mary," featured four classic *Mary Tyler Moore Show* episodes.

When The Walt Disney Company acquired 20th Century Fox in 2019, they also got the MTM library, including *The Mary Tyler Moore Show*. All seven seasons of the show are available to stream on Hulu, the streaming service owned by Disney.

In 2013, an episode of *Hot in Cleveland*, which starred Betty White and featured her *Mary Tyler Moore Show* costar Georgia Engel, did an MTM reunion with Moore, Valerie Harper, and Cloris Leachman. At the end of the episode, which was titled "Love Is All Around," the camera pans to a cat in the window—perhaps Mimsie meowing goodbye from beyond.

LIFE LESSON:
Know When It's Time for Goodbye

You know the first rule of show business? Leave them wanting more. That's why *The Mary Tyler Moore Show* team decided sometime during the sixth season to end the show in its seventh season while it was still in top form and still faring well in the ratings. "We thought, *Let's get off the air while we're still welcome in everybody's house. Let's go off while people were sorry to see us go,*" Burns later said. There was also the reality that the actors' contracts were due to expire, and they were being courted for other projects.

Moore told *Los Angeles Magazine* at the time that she was ready to move on to new challenges. "When you play the same character for seven years, you know all the facets, all the techniques, and once you reach that niche, it's time to go on. It's just not as challenging as it was in the beginning." Years later, Moore confessed that she could have gone on playing Mary Richards for longer, but she agreed to be a good sport and let the show end since that's what everyone else seemed to want. That's such a Mary Richards thing to do!

Show creators don't always have the chance to plan a show's ending, and this way, they could guarantee time to wrap things up the way they wanted to. In the last two seasons of the show, they managed to bring a number of ongoing story lines to satisfying, if not uniformly happy, conclusions. After countless marriage proposals, Georgette finally presses the issue, and she and Ted marry in an impromptu ceremony at Mary's apartment. The new couple struggles with infertility and are told they can't have biological children. They adopt a son, David, who is played by Robbie Rist, best known to classic TV fans as Cousin Oliver on *The Brady Bunch*. They then discover that . . . what do you know? Georgette is pregnant! She gives birth to a daughter they name Mary Lou after Mary and Lou help deliver her in Mary's bedroom! Murray and Marie have their fourth child, a son they adopt from Vietnam.

But *how* to end after seven years on the air? America had gotten to know Mary and her friends so well that saying goodbye would be heartbreaking. To craft this final episode, show creators Allan Burns and James L. Brooks invited every writer who had written on the show more than once to contribute. The all-star team they assembled included Ed Weinberger, Stan Daniels, David Lloyd, and Bob Ellison. Together, along with Burns and Brooks, they wrote a script that, as Brooks said, "Made the series end honestly." For Moore, ending the series honestly meant not marrying Mary Richards off.

Just like Mary herself, the producers never seemed to find just the right match for Mary. The only potential love match they saw involved Mary ending up with Lou Grant. The producers were open to the idea of having them couple up at the end of the show. "We thought it would be interesting to get a Tracy-Hepburn thing going out," Burns recalled. "It was not too far-fetched to us. But it was one of the few times Mary ever told us she couldn't get behind one of our ideas. She said no, so we wrote the episode where they tried to kiss instead." For Moore, there was never a question about it. Mary Richards would end the show single.

"To have Mary Richards get married and live happily ever after would be to turn our backs on all we've said on this show and all the good we've done," Moore told the audience before one of the show's final tapings in 1976. "Society says marriage is the ultimate goal, and it is the most wonderful state for many people—it certainly is for me—but it's not for everyone. In terms of asserting the right of a woman to be single and to have a career, we've said a lot in this show, and I wouldn't want to undo it now."

Instead of marrying Mary off, the writers decided on a different concept for the series finale. In "The Last Show," WJM-TV is sold, and the new station manager fires everyone *except* for Ted—a barbed commentary on the state of local news. Everyone's devastated—but especially Mary. Without her newsroom family, what will Mary do? Luckily, she's got Mr. Grant, who's really a big softie looking out for her. It seems he's spent all $800 of the office's petty cash to fly Rhoda in from New York and Phyllis in from San Francisco to cheer Mary up. Once they arrive, they end up competing to see who does a better job of comforting Mary. Typical frenemy behavior. "Hey, listen, guys, don't worry . . . It's going to be okay." Mary reassures them. But like the good friends they are, they can tell Mary is putting on a brave act for them.

"Mary, we didn't come a collective three thousand miles to watch you keep a stiff upper lip. Go ahead, feel bad if you want," says Rhoda.

"We're here for you. If you feel good, feel good. But if you feel sad, c'mon, just let it go."

At that, Mary cries, "Oh, Rhoda," and sobs into Rhoda's arms, until Phyllis wants a turn and Mary cries into her arms too.

During their last day in the newsroom, Mary seems lost. "Oh, Mr. Grant, what's the news matter anyway? It's our last day together." She tries to make a speech to the newsroom, but Mr. Grant puts her off. Why get unnecessarily sentimental? Let's hold off on the tears. "I don't want to see anyone moping around here," he barks at Murray and Mary.

Sue Ann sweeps into the newsroom with good news. It seems she's got a job, but "it's hard to explain." It involves an "elderly gentleman who is taking a cruise to the Mediterranean. I'll be traveling with him as sort of a 'practical nurse.'" Of course, Murray, as usual, has a snarky comeback: "That ought to be a nice change for you, Sue Ann, cruising at sea."

Ted presents a goofy, but well-intentioned, on-air farewell to his friends. "Last night, as I lay awake in my bed, I wondered how do I tell these dear friends and colleagues how I feel about them," he says before concluding with a line from the World War I–era marching song "It's a Long Way to Tipperary." As silly as Ted's tribute is, the significance of the occasion finally sinks in for Lou, and he starts to tear up. "Don't you realize this is the last time we'll all see this room?"

Mary goes to hug him, and as Lou looks at his newsroom friends with tears in his eyes, he begins a tear-jerking speech. He begins it but never finishes it because he's too broken up to speak: "I cherish you people." The entire group begins to cry and encircle Mary and Lou in a group hug. The characters, as well as the actors playing them, are crying so much that Lou says, "I think we all need some Kleenex." The script had specified: "They break up and they go to the Kleenex." But during rehearsal, Jim Brooks suggested they try to shuffle over together, staying in a hug the whole time. The teary group shuffle to reach the tissue box on Mary's desk became almost as iconic as Mary's initial hat toss.

Then, once they've all wiped their noses, Mary finally manages to give her speech: "I just wanted you to know that sometimes I get concerned about being a career woman. I get to thinking my job is too important to me, and I tell myself that the people I work with are just the people I work with. And not my family. And last night, I thought what is a family anyway? They're just people who make you feel less alone and really loved. And that's what you've done for me. Thank you for being my family."

"Now for the hard part. How do we leave this room?" Murray asks.

"That's not so hard," says Lou. "Remember what Ted said?" And he breaks out into the song Ted quoted on-air, "It's a Long Way to Tipperary." The gang all joins in, and arm in arm, they march out of the room weeping. Mary turns for one final look at the newsroom. Her eyes fill with tears, but the ever-plucky Mary Richards manages one final smile as she exits for the last time.

Apparently, the crew member in charge of dimming the set was so teary that he forgot to slip the lighting switch, and they had to shoot that part of the scene again.

After the characters on the show bid farewell to each other, the actors broke character and Moore introduced them to the audience, which mostly consisted of friends, family, and people who had worked on the show, as "the best cast ever." On March 19, 1977, the cast of *The Mary Tyler Moore Show* took their final bow.

On the occasion of the show's final taping, the *New York Times* hailed it as "one of television's best-written comedies" by saying it "laid to rest the myth that audiences would not accept a situation comedy involving a woman unless she was married and burned dinner at least one night a week."

LIFE LESSON:
Be a Role Model

What better way to lead than by example? The show was groundbreaking not only for its portrayal of a woman in the workplace but also for helping to create the new ubiquitous sitcom subgenre, the workplace comedy, or the working-woman sitcom. Without *The Mary Tyler Moore Show* blazing the trail for single professional women in prime time, we might not have had *Murphy Brown, Ally McBeal, Sex and the City, 30 Rock,* or *Girls.* So many show creators acknowledged *The Mary Tyler Moore Show* as an inspiration.

While developing *30 Rock,* actor/producer Tina Fey said she studied DVDs of *The Mary Tyler Moore Show.* "We talked about that show a lot as a template, obviously, of a great show but also a show that is all about the relationships in the workplace, but not the making of television so much," Fey told the *New York Times* back in 2007, after ending the show's debut season with a best comedy Emmy. There were certainly some obvious parallels between the two shows. Like *The Mary Tyler Moore Show*, *30 Rock* revolved around a thirtysomething single TV producer. Like Mary, Liz Lemon (Fey) has to deal with a gruff, sarcastic, but ultimately lovable boss, Jack Donaghy (Alec Baldwin), and a ridiculous colleague, a clueless TV star (Tracy Morgan). Liz's relationship with Jack is similar to the dynamic Mary and Lou shared. Both Mary and Liz ditch loser boyfriends and go on a zillion unsuccessful dates. Liz is notably more slovenly and less of a lady than Mary Richards. But, like Mary, she's got spunk.

The same is true for Kimmy Schmidt (Ellie Kemper), the plucky twenty-nine-year-old lead character of *Unbreakable Kimmy Schmidt*, the award-winning Netflix sitcom created by Fey and *30 Rock* showrunner Robert Carlock. Like Mary, Kimmy is a single woman with a sunny disposition who is determined to make it on her own in the big city with a quirky self-made family. Carlock acknowledged that with *Kimmy Schmidt* they wanted to "do the kind of 'Mary Tyler Moore' template of the girl in the big city."

Before *Kimmy Schmidt* and *30 Rock*, there was *Murphy Brown*, another witty, character-driven ensemble comedy centered around a single female newswoman. That show's creator, Diane English, said she had only seen a handful of episodes of *The Mary Tyler Moore Show*. Still, it's easy to picture Murphy Brown as an extension of Mary Richards, a smart, professional woman making it on her own in a newsroom full of colorful characters.

Amy Poehler's perky do-gooder Leslie Knope on the NBC sitcom *Parks and Recreation* shares character traits with Mary Richards. Just as Mary seeks advice from Mr. Grant, Leslie looks to her boss, Ron Swanson (Nick Offerman), for guidance in life. Both characters are hardworking and optimistic and earn the respect of their grouchy bosses. Poehler recognized the parallels, saying that Ron and Leslie have a "Mary-and-Lou-Grant kind of relationship."

In 2017, Lena Dunham, creator, writer, and star of *Girls*, wrote a tribute to *The Mary Tyler Moore Show* in *The New Yorker* in which she acknowledged that show's influence on her own. In *Girls*, Lena Dunham plays struggling twentysomething writer Hannah Horvath, who tries to "make it on her own" (well, with some help from her parents) in New York City. "When I was a young adult trying to create a television show about the messy business of femininity, *The Mary Tyler Moore Show* became a master class, the kind of viewing that made you both want to strive for the show's level of excellence and give up because they'd nailed the algorithm," wrote Dunham, who said she kept a small, framed architectural map of Mary Richard's apartment in her dressing room on the set of *Girls* as inspiration.

While Mary Richards smiled and tossed her beret in the air gleefully in the opening credits of *The Mary Tyler Moore Show*, *Sex and the City*'s Carrie Bradshaw (Sarah Jessica Parker) is splashed with water when a bus hits a puddle in the opening credits. In that show, Carrie is an updated version of Mary, a thirtysomething single woman trying to make it on her own with the help of friends. She deals with some of the same dating indignities that Mary does—for example, they both try dating twentysomething guys and have lots of disastrous dates. Of course, since Carrie appeared on HBO more than two decades after *The Mary Tyler Moore Show* went off the air, she and her girlfriends were much more explicit about their sex lives than Mary, Rhoda, and Phyllis ever were!

Crazy Ex-Girlfriend creator Rachel Bloom, who wrote and played the lead role of Rebecca Bunch on the CW musical-comedy series about a single woman in her early thirties navigating love and career, acknowledged the influence of *The Mary Tyler Moore Show*. "That idea of a plucky, conflicted ingenue who was adorable but still very conflicted and had problems of her own and was a deep, nuanced person—that really relates to our show," Bloom said.

The Mary Tyler Moore Show is the first sitcom to have an official series finale. Before that, sitcoms just ended without any special episode. In that way, and others, the show set the bar for future series finales. Before creating the last episode of *Friends*, the series creators, David Crane, Marta Kauffman, and Kevin S. Bright, reviewed finales from other sitcoms they admired, noting what worked and what didn't. "The ones we really like are the ones that stayed true to what the series was," Kauffman said. Crane agreed: "*Mary Tyler Moore*, that's the gold standard." In May 2019, *USA Today* ranked *The Mary Tyler Moore Show* fourth-best series finale of all time. "Just thinking about that loving final hug is enough to make any MTM fan tear up," wrote *USA Today*. "The finale ended in the sad, inescapable way many jobs in the real world do. The new owner of WJM fired the entire TV newsroom (well, except Ted), and the former coworkers came together to say goodbye. It felt realistic and emotional, just like most of the series' run." The finale also earned the writers yet another Emmy.

In 2002, a statue of Mary Richards tossing her hat was unveiled in downtown Minneapolis. Fans, including Tina Fey and Oprah Winfrey, continue to make the pilgrimage.

LIFE LESSON:
You're Gonna Make It After All

The show had made it after all, and so did the amazing cast, who continued to find meaningful work after the show ended. Mary Tyler Moore earned an Academy Award nomination for her role in Robert Redford's 1980 film *Ordinary People*, in which she played a very un-Mary-like mother coping with the accidental death of a son. She appeared in numerous plays and TV shows over the years, earning a Tony Award in 1980 for her performance as the quadriplegic lead character in the Broadway revival of *Whose Life Is It Anyway?* Incidentally, the part was originally written for a man. Once again, Moore was pushing boundaries.

Though she tried to return to sitcoms in the 1980s and 1990s, including shows like *Mary*, *Annie McGuire*, and *New York News*, those efforts were short-lived. She had more success with TV movies, winning her seventh Emmy for her supporting role as the ruthless owner of a 1940s Tennessee adoption agency in the Lifetime cable movie *Stolen Babies* in 1993. She played another memorably un-Mary-like character in the 2001 CBS movie *Like Mother Like Son: The Strange Story of Sante and Kenny Kimes*, about a true-life mother-son grifter pair who murder a New York socialite. *Variety* didn't like the movie much, but they noted that Moore had finally shed the Mary Richards image, saying she "has gone from the woman who could turn the world on with a smile to the woman who can creep you out with just one look." She was memorably cast as Ben Stiller's mother, who shows off her bra in the 1996 indie film *Flirting with Disaster*. In 2012, she received the Screen Actors Guild Lifetime Achievement Award, which was presented to her by Dick Van Dyke. Moore died in 2017 at the age of eighty.

Since playing gruff producer Lou Grant in *The Mary Tyler Moore Show* and the award-winning *Lou Grant* spin-off about a newspaper city editor, Ed Asner hasn't slowed down. He served as the president of the Screen Actors Guild from 1981 to 1985. In addition to appearing in films such as Oliver Stone's *JFK*, Asner has worked as a voice artist for countless movies and TV series, including *The Cleveland Show* and Pixar's *Up*. Asner holds the record for being the man with the most Primetime Emmy Awards for acting, with seven in total.

Notably, he is one of only two actors to win an Emmy Award for both comedy and drama for the same role, though the drama Emmy was for the MTM spin-off *Lou Grant*. *Orange Is the New Black*'s Uzo Aduba also won an Emmy for both comedy and drama for her role of Suzanne "Crazy Eyes" Warren. Asner continues to work steadily, including guest appearances on the Emmy Award–winning sitcom *Modern Family* and Netflix's *Grace and Frankie*. In a riff on his Lou Grant character, Asner voiced the editor of the *Springfield Shopper* newspaper, who hires Homer as a critic on *The Simpsons*.

Before *The Mary Tyler Moore Show* ended, Gavin MacLeod signed on to take the helm of *The Love Boat* as Captain Merrill Stubing, who gets far more respect than Murray Slaughter ever did. During the nine seasons the show was on the air, most of MacLeod's former *Mary Tyler Moore Show* colleagues hopped aboard as guest stars, including Betty White, Ted Knight, Valerie Harper, Cloris Leachman, and Georgia Engel. Nancy Walker and Harold Gould, who had played Rhoda's parents on *The Mary Tyler Moore Show*, also came aboard *The Love Boat*, as did John Amos, who had played Gordy on the show. MacLeod, eighty-nine years old as of this writing, has since guest starred on a number of comedies, including *That '70s Show*, *The King of Queens*, and Disney Channel's *The Suite Life on Deck*. In 2000, MacLeod played a cardinal on HBO's prison drama *Oz*, which was created by Tom Fontana, who got his start writing for MTM Enterprises's *St. Elsewhere*.

Valerie Harper left *The Mary Tyler Moore Show* for a spin-off titled *Rhoda*, which ran from 1974 to 1978. She starred in the short-lived sitcom *Valerie* in the mid-1980s and, later, made guest appearances on a number of shows, including *Desperate Housewives* and *The Office*. In 1998, Harper played an Italian mother on *Melrose Place*, and the following year, she was a Rhoda-style Jewish mother who bonds with Carrie Bradshaw (Sarah Jessica Parker) on *Sex and the City*. After learning she had terminal cancer in 2013, Harper competed on *Dancing with the Stars*. Harper voiced characters in the Adult Swim show *Children's Hospital*, *American Dad!*, and *The Simpsons*, produced by her old *Mary Tyler Moore Show* producer James L. Brooks. Harper died in 2019 at age eighty.

The Ted Knight Show had a six-episode run in 1978 before going off the air. In 1980, Knight starred alongside Rodney Dangerfield, Chevy Chase, and Bill Murray in the cult comedy *Caddyshack*. That same year, he landed the role of Henry Rush, a married cartoonist and overprotective father whose grown daughters move into his San Francisco duplex in *Too Close for Comfort*. The show was later revamped and retitled *The Ted Knight Show*, which would have returned for another season, except for Knight's colon cancer. He died in 1986 at sixty-two.

Betty White received Emmy nominations for the part of naive widow Rose Nyland on *The Golden Girls* (1985–1992) seven years in a row, and won once. White also won Emmys for guest appearances on *The John Larroquette Show* and *Saturday Night Live*, in addition to the two she won for *The Mary Tyler Moore Show*. She also appeared in more than one hundred episodes of the TV Land comedy *Hot in Cleveland*, which ran for six seasons, ending in 2015. White, ninety-eight as of this writing, is more popular than ever and continues to work. Having made her TV debut in 1939, she holds the record for the longest TV career by an entertainer (female), according to *The Guinness Book of World Records*.

After being cast as Phyllis on *The Mary Tyler Moore Show*, Leachman's career took off. While she was still on the show, in 1971, Leachman won an Academy Award for Best Supporting Actress for her performance in *The Last Picture Show*, the Peter Bogdanovich film adapted from the bestselling Larry McMurtry book of the same name. Just a few years later, in 1974, Leachman made audiences laugh in Mel Brooks's *Young Frankenstein*, the first of three times she'd work with the great comic director. She also starred in the spin-off *Phyllis*, which ran for two seasons. She had a recurring role as Beverly Ann Stickle in *The Facts of Life*, as well as many TV guest spots and film appearances. She played the despicable Grandma Ida on *Malcolm in the Middle* from 2001 to 2006 and Maw Maw on *Raising Hope* until 2014. She also appeared on the seventh season of *Dancing with the Stars*, making her, at eighty-two, the oldest person to ever compete on the show. She has won eight Emmys for acting, a record that Julia Louis-Dreyfus tied in 2019. She appears in the reboot of *Mad About You*.

After *The Mary Tyler Moore Show* ended, Georgia Engel was a regular on costar Betty White's short-lived sitcom *The Betty White Show* and made guest appearances on a number of shows, including *The Love Boat, Fantasy Island*, and, much later, *Two and a Half Men*. Engel had a recurring role on *Coach* and received three consecutive Emmy nominations for outstanding guest star in a comedy for her role as Robert

Barone's (Brad Garrett) mother-in-law on the sitcom *Everybody Loves Raymond*. She voiced characters in numerous animated films, including three *Open Season* films and *The Care Bears Movie*. She played the role of Mamie, Betty White's character's best friend in *Hot in Cleveland*. Her final credited TV appearance was in Netflix's reboot of *One Day at a Time*. She died in 2019 at age seventy.

Over the years, CBS produced two specials commemorating the show, *Mary Tyler Moore: The 20th Anniversary Show* in 1991 and *The Mary Tyler Moore Reunion* in 2002. In 2008, the surviving cast members reunited on *The Oprah Winfrey Show*. Winfrey had her staff re-create the sets of the WJM-TV newsroom and Mary's original apartment. Moore and Harper reprised their roles in a two-hour ABC TV movie, *Mary and Rhoda*, which aired on ABC in 2000.

An extraordinary list of postgraduate success speaks well of an institution. *Mary Tyler Moore* alumni continued to entertain us over the years in ways that showed us that while the magic of *The Mary Tyler Moore Show* was a singular event, they all had a little magic of their own. Looking back on the show, Moore felt content with the legacy she had left behind. "Very few of us are lucky enough to, at the end of our life, know we were here for some purpose," she said. "And I am going to be one of those lucky few. I know I served some people very well."

ACKNOWLEDGMENTS

This book wouldn't exist without the imagination and foresight of my editor, Jennifer Kasius, or the support of my agent and friend, Peter Steinberg. It also wouldn't have been possible without the love and encouragement of my family and friends. Endless thanks to my husband, Anthony Orkin, for supplying me with oat lattes, dark chocolate, and delicious home-cooked meals, as well as helpful editorial input and lots of love. Thanks to my mother, Marilyn Bernstein, and my late father, Bernie Bernstein, for their unconditional love and support and for encouraging me to pursue my dreams. All those hours watching TV as a kid paid off!

I have enormous respect for the creators, producers, writers, actors, and everyone who was involved with *The Mary Tyler Moore Show*. Even all these years later, the remarkable show they created continues to resonate with viewers. So much of this book is a tribute to their wit, talent, and insight, so I owe them a great deal of gratitude. Having taken a deep dive into all things related to the show, I have gained immense admiration for the authors whose footsteps I've followed, including Jennifer Keishin Armstrong, Robert S. Alley, and Irby B. Brown.

There were times during the writing process when I doubted I could do *The Mary Tyler Moore Show* justice. Thanks to friends Janet Morgan, Nathalie Jacqmotte, Jessica Rhys, Diane Avenoso, Beth Federici, Jackie Weissman, Samantha Parton, and the gang at Oui Presse, who cheered me on, brought me treats, and reminded me to take a break from the computer. Thanks also to dear old friends Dori Fern and Blair Miller, whose pep talks helped buoy me when I needed it most.

Finally, thanks to my amazing daughters, Jess and Ruby, for putting up with my nonstop Mary Tyler Moore references and, more importantly, for inspiring me every day. I love you!

ENDNOTES

CHAPTER ONE:
Opportunity

The Mary Tyler Moore Show, "Love Is All Around," season 1, episode 1

Bianculli, David, *The Platinum Age of Television: From I Love Lucy to the Walking Dead* (Anchor Books, 2017)

How Mary Tyler Moore Made Minneapolis a Star, MPR News, January 25, 2017

The Story Behind the Iconic 'Mary Tyler Moore Show' Opening, ABC News.com, January 27, 2017

Mary Tyler Moore interview with the Television Academy Foundation, October 23, 1997

Armstrong, Jennifer Keishin, *Mary and Lou and Rhoda and Ted: And All the Brilliant Minds Who Made* The Mary Tyler Moore Show *a Classic* (Simon & Schuster, 2013)

Harper, Valerie, *I, Rhoda: A Memoir* (Gallery Books, 2013)

"Don't Look Now, but TV Is Growing Up," *New York Times*, May 20, 1973

"The Story of How 'Love Is All Around' Became the Theme to 'The Mary Tyler Moore Show,'" *Los Angeles Times*, January 27, 2017

"Mary Tyler Moore and the Company That Changed America," *Observer*, February 9, 2017

The Mary Tyler Moore Show season 1 DVD supplemental materials

"Our Q&A with 'Mary Tyler Moore Show' Writer Susan Silver," *Milwaukee Magazine*, June 19, 2017

"The Silverman Strategy," *New York Times*, March 7, 1976

Silver, Susan, "How Mary Tyler Moore Revolutionized TV for Female Writers Like Me," *Refinery 29*, January 26, 2017

"Fall Preview," *TV Guide*, September 12, 1970

"Comedies Appear Back to Back," *St. Petersburg Times*, September 19, 1970

"The New Season: Perspiring with Relevance," *Time*, September 29, 1970

"Let's Hope First Impressions Are Deceiving," *New York Times*, September 27, 1970

CHAPTER TWO:

Family

The Mary Tyler Moore Show, "The Last Show," season 7, episode 24

The Mary Tyler Moore Show, "Support Your Local Mother," season 1, episode 6

The Mary Tyler Moore Show, "The Lou and Edie Story," season 4, episode 4

Mary Tyler Moore interview with the Television Academy Foundation, October 23, 1997

Allan Burns interview with the Television Academy Foundation, February 18, 2004

Ethel Winant interview with the Television Academy Foundation, August 7, 1996

Harper, Valerie, *I, Rhoda: A Memoir* (Gallery Books, 2013)

Alley, Robert S., and Irby B. Brown, *Love Is All Around: The Making of* The Mary Tyler Moore Show (Dell Publishing, 1989)

"The On and Off Screen Connection Between Mary Tyler Moore and Ed Asner," Biography.com, January 3, 2020

The Mary Tyler Moore Show season 1 DVD supplemental materials

"Remembering Grant Tinker, 'Mary Tyler Moore' Producer and NBC Chair," NPR's *Fresh Air*, December 15, 2016

CHAPTER THREE:
Friends

═══════

The Mary Tyler Moore Show, "Love Is All Around," season 1, episode 1

The Mary Tyler Moore Show, "Today I Am a Ma'am," season 1, episode 2

The Mary Tyler Moore Show, "Bess, You Is My Daughter Now," season 1, episode 3

The Mary Tyler Moore Show, "Divorce Isn't Everything," season 1, episode 4

The Mary Tyler Moore Show, "Some of My Best Friends Are Rhoda," season 2, episode 23

The Mary Tyler Moore Show, "The Georgette Story," season 3, episode 18

The Mary Tyler Moore Show, "Put on a Happy Face," season 3, episode 23

The Mary Tyler Moore Show, "The Lars Affair," season 4, episode 1

The Mary Tyler Moore Show, "Best of Enemies," season 4, episode 19

The Mary Tyler Moore Show, "Mary Richards: Producer," season 5, episode 16

The Mary Tyler Moore Show, "What Do You Want to Do When You Produce," season 6, episode 15

"Opposites Do Attract . . . When Making Friends," *DailyMail.com*, August 9, 2016

Allan Burns interview with the Television Academy Foundation, February 18, 2004

Valerie Harper interview with the Television Academy Foundation, February 26, 2009

Mary Tyler Moore interview with the Television Academy Foundation, October 23, 1997

"Valerie Harper Tackles Tallulah Bankhead," NPR's *Talk of the Nation*, May 25, 2010

"MTM and Her All-Star Team," *Newsweek*, January 29, 1973

"After 25 Years, the 'Real' Betty White," *Los Angeles Times*, December 21, 1973.

CHAPTER FOUR:

Work

The Mary Tyler Moore Show, "Love Is All Around," season 1, episode 1

The Mary Tyler Moore Show, "The Boss Isn't Coming for Dinner," season 1, episode 21

The Mary Tyler Moore Show, "I Gave at the Office," season 4, episode 13

The Mary Tyler Moore Show, "The Snow Must Go On," season 1, episode 8

The Mary Tyler Moore Show, "The 45-Year-Old Man," season 1, episode 24

The Mary Tyler Moore Show, "The Good Time News," season 3, episode 1

The Mary Tyler Moore Show, "Hi There, Sports Fans," season 4, episode 5

The Mary Tyler Moore Show, "Will Mary Richards Go to Jail?," season 5, episode 1

The Mary Tyler Moore Show, "Mary Richards: Producer," season 5, episode 16

The Mary Tyler Moore Show, "Anyone Who Hates Kids and Dogs," season 5, episode 24

The Mary Tyler Moore Show, "What's Wrong with Swimming," season 7, episode 4

"John Amos on *Mary Tyler Moore*, Racism on Set, and Playing the First Black Family Man," *Vulture*, October 13, 2015

CHAPTER FIVE:
Home

The Mary Tyler Moore Show, "The Dinner Party," season 4, episode 10

The Mary Tyler Moore Show, "Mary Moves Out," season 6, episode 2

"The Mary Tyler Moore Show Apartment Was the Epitome of Single Girl Cool," *Apartment Therapy*, January 25, 2017

"Homeowners Grew Weary of Mary Tyler Moore Attention 45 Years Ago," *WSTP Eyewitness News*, May 25, 2018

"Just Listed: The Former 'Mary Tyler Moore House,'" *StarTribune*, December 20, 2012

"How Mary Tyler Moore Show Shaped American Working Women's Style," *Hollywood Reporter*, January 27, 2017

Harper, Valerie, *I, Rhoda: A Memoir* (Gallery Books, 2013)

"Isaac Mizrahi Remembers a TV and Fashion Icon," *W Magazine*, January 29, 2017

"Mindfulness: The New Science of Health and Happiness: Try New Things," *Time Magazine 2017 Special Edition*

CHAPTER SIX:
Feminism

═══════

The Mary Tyler Moore Show, "A Son for Murray," season 5, episode 12

"Celebrating the Life of a TV Pioneer," *People Commemorative Edition, Mary Tyler Moore 1936–2017*

The Mary Tyler Moore Show, "I Gave at the Office," season 4, episode 13

The Mary Tyler Moore Show, "Who's in Charge Here?," season 3, episode 3

The Mary Tyler Moore Show, "Rhoda the Beautiful," season 3, episode 6

The Mary Tyler Moore Show, "Mary's Aunt," season 6, episode 6

The Mary Tyler Moore Show, "Mary's Aunt Returns," season 6, episode 21

"How Nora Ephron Said Goodbye to *The Mary Tyler Moore Show*," *Esquire*, January 25, 2017

Mary Tyler Moore Show season 1 DVD supplemental materials

"Hazel Frederick Dies at 91," *AP*, November 30, 1999

Mary Tyler Moore interview with the Television Academy Foundation, October 23, 1997

"TV Pioneer Brings Fun to Films," *Los Angeles Times*, June 21, 2009

"Comedy Writer Treva Silverman," Television Academy, December 10, 2013

Diahann Carroll on *Pioneers of Television: Breaking Barriers*, PBS, April 29, 2014

Marlo Thomas interview with the Television Academy Foundation, March 26, 2003

CHAPTER SEVEN:
Humor

The Mary Tyler Moore Show, "Anchorman Overboard," season 1, episode 12

The Mary Tyler Moore Show, "He's No Heavy . . . He's My Brother," season 2, episode 3

The Mary Tyler Moore Show, "My Brother's Keeper," season 3, episode 17

The Mary Tyler Moore Show, "What Are Friends For?," season 5, episode 10

The Mary Tyler Moore Show, "An Affair to Forget," season 5, episode 15

The Mary Tyler Moore Show, "Phyllis Whips Inflation," season 5, episode 18

The Mary Tyler Moore Show, "Ted's Moment of Glory," season 6, episode 5

The Mary Tyler Moore Show, "Chuckles Bites the Dust," season 6, episode 7

The Mary Tyler Moore Show, "Mary Midwife," season 7, episode 1

Alley, Robert S., and Irby B. Brown, *Love Is All Around: The Making of The Mary Tyler Moore Show* (Dell Publishing, 1989)

"How Nora Ephron Said Goodbye to *The Mary Tyler Moore Show*," *Esquire*, January 25, 2017

Harper, Valerie, *I, Rhoda: A Memoir* (Gallery Books, 2013)

"How Nora Ephron Said Goodbye to *The Mary Tyler Moore Show*," *Esquire*, January 25, 2017

Oprah.com, "Love Is All Around," https://www.oprah.com/oprahshow/the-cast-of-the-mary-tyler-moore-show-reunites_1/all

"What Julia Louis-Dreyfus Loves about Mary Tyler Moore," *Entertainment Weekly*, November 24, 2006

"Michelle Obama Interview: How FLOTUS Used Pop Culture Stardom to Make an Impact," *Variety*, August 23, 2016

CHAPTER EIGHT:

Kindness

The Mary Tyler Moore Show, "Thoroughly Unmilitant Mary," season 2, episode 8

The Mary Tyler Moore Show, "It's Whether You Win or Lose," season 3, episode 5

The Mary Tyler Moore Show, "Murray Faces Life," season 3, episode 21

The Mary Tyler Moore Show, "Lou's First Date," season 4, episode 8

The Mary Tyler Moore Show, "Ted's Change of Heart," season 7, episode 5

The Mary Tyler Moore Show, "Murray Can't Lose," season 7, episode 10

Alley, Robert S., and Irby B. Brown, *Love Is All Around: The Making of* The Mary Tyler Moore Show (Dell Publishing, 1989)

"Being Kind to Others Does Make You 'Slightly Happier,'" University of Oxford, October 5, 2016

CHAPTER NINE:
Love and Sex

═══════════

The Mary Tyler Moore Show, "1040 or Fight," season 1, episode 11

The Mary Tyler Moore Show, "The Birds and the . . . um . . . Bees," season 2, episode 1

The Mary Tyler Moore Show, "The Good-Time News," season 3, episode 1

The Mary Tyler Moore Show, "Just Around the Corner," season 3, episode 7

The Mary Tyler Moore Show, "The Courtship of Mary's Father's Daughter," season 3, episode 15

The Mary Tyler Moore Show, "Remembrance of Things Past," season 3, episode 22

The Mary Tyler Moore Show, "Angels in the Snow," season 4, episode 2

The Mary Tyler Moore Show, "Lou and That Woman," season 5, episode 4

The Mary Tyler Moore Show, "What Are Friends For?," season 5, episode 10

The Mary Tyler Moore Show, "Mary's Delinquent," season 6, episode 8

The Mary Tyler Moore Show, "Once I Had a Secret Love," season 6, episode 18

The Mary Tyler Moore Show, "Mary Midwife," season 7, episode 1

The Mary Tyler Moore Show, "Sue Ann's Sister," season 7, episode 3

The Mary Tyler Moore Show, "Mary's Three Husbands," season 7, episode 21

The Mary Tyler Moore Show, "Lou Dates Mary," season 7, episode 23

Armstrong, Jennifer Keishin, *Mary and Lou and Rhoda and Ted: And All the Brilliant Minds Who Made* The Mary Tyler Moore Show *a Classic* (Simon & Schuster, 2013)

"TV's Reigning Queen," *People*, September 30, 1974

Alley, Robert S., and Irby B. Brown, *Love Is All Around: The Making of* The Mary Tyler Moore Show (Dell Publishing, 1989)

"After 25 Years, the 'Real' Betty White," *Los Angeles Times*, December 21, 1973

CHAPTER TEN:

Putting It All Together

The Mary Tyler Moore Show, "The Last Show," season 7, episode 24

The Peabody Awards Committee, 1977

Armstrong, Jennifer Keishin, *Mary and Lou and Rhoda and Ted: And All the Brilliant Minds Who Made* The Mary Tyler Moore Show *a Classic* (Simon & Schuster, 2013)

"Last Days of Mary Tyler Moore," *Los Angeles Magazine*, November 1976

"The Making of The Mary Tyler Moore Show: How the Late Actress Found—and Shaped—Her Iconic Role," *People*, January 25, 2017

Dunham, Lena, "Everything I Learned from Mary Tyler Moore," *The New Yorker*, January 27, 2017

Rosenberg, Howard, "'Mary and Rhoda': They May Yet Make It After All," *Los Angeles Times*, February 7, 2000

Allan Burns interview with the Television Academy Foundation, February 18, 2004

Mary Tyler Moore interview with the Television Academy Foundation, October 23, 1997

"Lena Thwaite Really Wants to Make a Biopic of Mary Tyler Moore," *Time*, April 2, 2018

"Your Favorite TV Show Probably Owes a Debt to Mary Tyler Moore," *Washington Post*, January 26, 2017

"'30 Rock' Lives, and Tina Fey Laughs," *New York Times*, September 23, 2007

"The Best and Worst TV Series Finales of All Time," *USA Today*, May 20, 2019

"Tina Fey and Robert Carlock Talk 'Unbreakable Kimmy Schmidt,'" *Entertainment Weekly*, January 7, 2015

"Mary Tyler Moore at Series End Can Now Savor Its Innovations," *New York Times*, February 3, 1977

"'Friends' Challenge—Finding Right Words to Say Goodbye," *SF Gate*, January 14, 2004

"Like Mother Like Son: The Strange Story of Sante and Kenny Kimes," *Variety*, May 15, 2001

"We Really Need a New Word for Binge-Watching," *Mashable*, January 27, 2019

Thompson, Robert, *Television's Second Golden Age: From Hill Street Blues to ER* (Syracuse University Press, 1997)

About the Author

——————

PAULA BERNSTEIN is a veteran entertainment journalist whose work has appeared in *Fortune, Fast Company, TV Guide, The New York Times,* and many other publications. She has held staff positions at *IndieWire, Variety,* and *The Hollywood Reporter*. She is the co-author of *Identical Strangers: A Memoir of Twins Separated and Reunited*. A native New Yorker, Bernstein lives in Portland, Oregon with her family. Visit her at paulabernstein.com.